the 6 Mosquitoes

that drain the life out of marriage and relationships

Steve and Debbie Wilson
with Shelley McMillian

This book is dedicated to our children Josh and Leigh, Jordan, JaNae and Shelley. Thank you for your encouragement and for sharing with us a will to persevere through the journeys of life. We are grateful we are sharing the journeys together. Thank you also for daily reminding us of what is truly important in life!

CONTENTS

INTRODUCTION

"I have set before you life and prosperity, death and destruction. Now choose life, so you and your children may love the Lord your God, listen to his voice and hold fast to Him."
~ Deuteronomy 30:15, 19

Are you looking for marriage tools that assist your marriage in being the absolute best it can be? Are you searching for tools that hit you where you live and reach into your heart to make long term change? Do any of the following questions sound familiar?

Why does he/she do those things?

Are we the only couple going through this?

How can I get him/her to listen to me?

Is it too late for healing in our marriage?

Why isn't this fun anymore?

If God made marriage and intended it for good, then why on earth does it seem to be so difficult?

If any of these questions hit home or if you have a great marriage and simply want to continue growing, this book is for you. This study will assist couples in identifying the obstacles and distractions that disconnect relationships. Marriages today are left vulnerable with weak spots that become susceptible to attack. This study will identify the things that work against us so that we may guard and protect the things that work for us. Reflection for Direction will allow you the opportunity to reflect on each topic and share your thoughts with one another at the end of each day of study. Life Talk is designed so that you may share this study within a Life or Community group while Choose Life will give you words to meditate on as you continue toward the future growth of your marriage and relationships.

Paul states in Ephesians 3:17-19, "And I pray that you, being rooted and established in love, along with the saints, could grasp how high and wide and long and deep is the love of God. And to know this love which surpasses all understanding, so you may be filled to the fullness of the measure of God." Is your marriage rooted and established in love? At the time we said "I do" we had the vision of a fairy tale of the life we were going to live. However, somewhere along the journey the roads began to look differently than the movies pictured them. While we are living the anticipation of the "All-American Dream" of white picket fences, 2.5 kids, unending romance and a guaranteed happily ever after, life is passing us by and relationships are losing connections.

In order to begin the reconnection process, we must first have a clear picture of where the All-American dream begins and ends. The All-American fairy tale begins and ends with a commitment to stay forever. It means that no matter what life brings-trials or triumphs, successes or sorrows, good times or bad times, love or loss-that I am committed to this one person whom God has joined me with for the rest of my life. It means that I will always take the road less traveled over the road with easy options. It means that I will choose grace over defense, patience over frustration, service over selfishness and ultimately, God's way over the world's way.

How then, you may ask, do we begin to make the right choices for the future growth of our marriage? Join us as we journey together to a place where love abounds and marriage is more than you ever dreamed it could be.

BUSYNESS ~ BALANCE

THE QUESTION I MUST ASK:

WHAT DO YOU PERCEIVE AS THE MOST
IMPORTANT THING
IN MY LIFE?

TOO DISTRACTED TO CONNECT

"When we get too caught up in the busyness of the world, we lose connection with one another – and ourselves." ~ Jack Kornfield

Busyness seems to rob us of so many things in life and we do not even recognize it. Have you ever woken up in the morning and before you knew it, it was time to go to bed and you had no recollection of what the day even consisted of? That is a common trait of a busy person. In order for us to accomplish certain goals throughout our day, we must first make the choice to decide what is truly important. It seems as though society continues to get faster and faster paced. While at work, many of you are probably worried about what is going on at home. Have I spent enough time with the children this week? Have I taken the time to encourage and communicate with my spouse? And while at home, many times our time is spent worrying about pressing matters we did not finish at the office. It seems, at times, like life is such a whirlwind that we do not even have enough time to stop and balance that which is of utmost importance.

What is a typical day in your life?

_____

_____

_____

Do you plan your day or does your day plan you?

_____

_____

_____

One of the greatest enemies of busyness is distraction. Have you ever begun a project, only to get distracted by a million different things? One morning Steve decided to clean the garage. While cleaning the garage, he decided the grass needed mowing so he left the garage and began mowing. While mowing the grass, he noticed that a tree limb was down so he grabbed the chain saw and began cutting. Three hours went by and I arrived home, only to say, "I thought you were going to clean the garage." This is a great visual of how we start our day off with good intentions of accomplishing something, only to let people, circumstances and distractions get us off task. If you are a multi-tasker or high achiever, your initial thought is, "wow, but look what all he got done." The problem with that is that what began as the goal for the day, finished with mediocre results because of the many distractions.

The visual is not much different than what happens in relationships. We begin our marriage with that relationship as our primary priority. We desire to be with our mate, grow with our mate and connect with our mate. One day we wake up and what was once our greatest desire has now become something we give so little of ourselves to as we unconsciously allow the busyness of life to distract us from our main goal.

What distractions can you identify that have taken you away from growing your marriage?

_____

_____

_____

What would you say are your top priorities?

_____

_____

_____

What do your actions say are your top priorities?

_____

_____

_____

We have a very good friend who is the Director of Hockey Operations and Head Coach for a professional hockey team. One evening, after reading through a book which asked him to name what he believed the most important thing in his life was, the book then asked him to go to his family and ask them what they felt was the most important thing in his life. He amassed the courage to do so and went to his children and asked, "What is the most important thing in Daddy's life?" Because of his great love for his children, he was expecting to hear, "me, Daddy". Instead, he was crushed to hear his children say "hockey!" You see, it does not matter what we say is important. We most show what is important to us by the things that get our time and attention.

Would you be willing to ask your family what they perceive is the most important thing to you? What do you think they would say?

_____

_____

_____

How, then, when there are so many things pulling for our time, do we change the course of our "busyness?"

Psalm 46:10 says, "Be still and know that I am God."

I believe that God knew there would be seasons in our lives when many things would be pulling at us and vying for our attention. In fact, those of us who can live the fast paced life of do, do, do are pretty popular by the world's standards. Have you ever stopped to think about what keeps you so busy? Are you seeking the approval of the world more than you are seeking the approval of God and your family or are you simply seeking ways to tune out the things that have made life so difficult? Busyness, if not reeled in, can be a drug that causes some of the same heart aches as alcohol and drugs. Now you may be thinking, come on, how can busyness even be relative to things that destroy families, relationships and careers? Many times the source of busyness isn't any different than the source of things that seem to be unacceptable addictions. And if we are not careful, many of us will be on our death bed regretting the fact that we were too busy to live the life God had planned for us and too busy to love the people God gave us to love.

How often are you still? Is it difficult to be still and quiet?

_____

_____

_____

If you stopped long enough to be still, what do you think God would say to you in the stillness?

_____

_____

_____

Reflection for Direction

From the time you wake up in the morning, busyness can strip you of the one thing that you MUST have to balance the busyness. Life forces are so strong and without realizing it, we have put our relationship with God on the back burner and allowed insignificant things to take our attention. The longer we do this, the easier it becomes to put that relationship aside. The good news is that God is constantly pursuing us and loving us back to Him, and because of this it is not too late for you to snuggle up to Him and begin again.

Life Talk

While it is difficult for many of us to share our vulnerabilities, our weaknesses and even our strengths, God created us to live life together. While it is scary for some personalities to share, the risks have unbelievably awesome rewards. How then can we begin to empower and encourage each other the way the disciples were taught to support and lean on one another? Let's begin by sharing 10 ways to balance the busyness of life.

Choose Life

"And this is my prayer: that your love may abound more and more in knowledge and depth of insight, so that you may be able to discern what is best and may be pure and blameless until the day of Christ."
~ Philippians 1:9

THE BALANCING ACT

"Be aware of wonder. Live a balanced life - learn some and think some and draw and paint and sing and dance and play and work every day some." ~ Robert Fulgham

When I initially think of balance, a juggler quickly comes to mind. A good juggler can keep many objects in the air at all times. But have you ever stopped to think about what makes a juggler good? First of all, he must stay focused on the discipline of keeping the objects in the air, the same way we must stay disciplined in order to maintain our relationship with God, a healthy home and a balanced career. In a juggler's world, if one object gets out of balance, so go all the objects. Our life is the same way. If we wake up in the morning and opt out of my time with God, it has the ability to change the focus of the entire day. However, if we have spent time with God and forget that we have the responsibility of maintaining a healthy home and the obligation of providing for my family then so goes a balanced life.

Can you identify all the objects you are currently juggling?

_____

_____

_____

Which of these objects could you let go of?

_____

_____

_____

From time to time, it would benefit all of us to take inventory of our lives. Steve and I were forced to do this at the twelve year mark. At the writing of this book, we are still realizing the facade that so many of us take into marriage that we, too, bought into for so long. The Christian world asks of us to awake each morning with the underlying expectation that we tuck what is going on in our personal lives into our file folder and leave it there until we are safely back behind the closed door of our home. So, for twelve years that is exactly what Steve and I did. To make it through, he devoured his life into his ministry and I devoured mine into shallow and unhealthy emotional connections. Our individual inventories looked something like this:

Debbie-I loved conflict and was in it to win it. Neither my father nor my brother protected me growing up and by gosh, I was going to test Steve to gauge his love and protection for me. I struggled with failure and because I felt as though I were failing in our marriage, my initial response was to quit. I walked in one night and said, "If this is what marriage is like, I'm out." I so deeply wounded Steve and my selfishness was on the brink of also wounding my children. I was too caught up in my own world to even stop and think about whom all my decisions would ultimately affect. It is tough even today to think of what life may be like for all of us had I left.

Ladies, what does the inventory of your marriage look like through your eyes?

_____

_____

_____

Steve-I did not have the tools to even begin to know what balance looked like. I was living life and feeling as though everything was great. We had a home, kids, a dog and a healthy sex life so what more could one woman want? When Debbie walked in that night, I felt as though I had received a 2x4 to my forehead. I could not figure out for the life of me what we could change. I had never loved anyone my entire life the way I loved Debbie, but I was forced to realize that I was not engaged emotionally with her.

Men, what does the inventory of your marriage look like through your eyes?

_____

_____

_____

At that twelve year mark when the walls began to cave in and we began to realize that we were dropping all objects we had been trying to juggle, we had a choice. We could either quit or bunker in and realize that sometimes the better in marriage comes after the worse. We were forced to get out of ourselves and for the first time in my life, I was forced to fight for something and Steve was forced to pull himself out of defeat. I had to begin the process of working through my failure and he had to be willing to sacrifice his career dreams for his family dreams.

Which of your personal dreams are you willing to give up for your family dreams?

_____

_____

_____

Which of your personal dreams are you willing to give up for your eternal dreams?

_____

_____

_____

Reflection for Direction

Too many times, we choose to give up time with our mate, our children and God because it is easy to hang onto the affirmations that the world gives us. It is never too late to begin the restoration process of acknowledging your wrong and pushing pride aside so that you may leave a legacy of love long after you are gone. Because God orders our steps, we can always be assured that there is enough time in each day to do His will. What is God asking you to do that you are replacing with insignificant things? "It is God who works in you to will and to act according to His good purpose." ~ Philippians 2:13

Life Talk

We recently counseled a man that stated, "When I die, I don't think my wife will miss me. I think she will miss my income and the things I do for her and the children. But I don't believe it will take her long to get over my funeral service." That is a sad thought! While we are still breathing air we should be living toward the legacy we want to leave for others. Are you investing your life in the people who will cry at your funeral? What exactly are you investing? Are you investing monetarily, materialistically or eternally? Are you giving your children things that will increase their life and love for the Lord? When you are gone, what is it you want people to say about you? Make the choice to live for those things.

Choose Life

"In all things we are more than conquerors through Him who loved us. For I am convinced that neither death nor life, neither angels nor demons, neither the present nor the future, nor any powers, neither height nor depth, nor anything else in all creation, will be able to separate us from the love of Christ." ~ Romans 8:37-39

FIRMLY FOCUS

"Our thoughts create our reality—where we put our focus is the direction we tend to go." ~ Peter McWilliams

We love tennis in our family. When one of the major grand slam tournaments is on, we are glued to it. I'm not sure why it's tennis that we love so much other than the amazing focus it takes to play the game. Who can remember Jimmy Connors and his great comeback in 1991 at the US Open? He was down 2 sets to love, down 5-2 in the third set and still won the match. Marriage is like that sometimes. There are certain times we find ourselves moving through what seems to be a smooth and easy trek and then other times we feel like our back is to the wall. Maybe it's a bill that comes in the mail, a child that gets sick, or a hateful word. Boom!! Before we know it, our focus has shifted off what is good and moved us to a place where Satan loves for us to live.

What things tend to knock you off course?

_____

_____

_____

Do you tend to be an optimist or a pessimist? Explain.

_____

_____

_____

If you are a person who sees the glass as half empty, you are going to tend to find the wrong in things. However, if you see the glass as half full, while you may bring a background to the table that was full of negativity, you are still able to turn everything in a positive direction and see the silver lining through even the darkest clouds. John Maxwell states in his workbook, <u>Winning With People</u> that we tend to see life through a Lens Principle. Basically our identity comes from our perspective on life and people which means that who we are determines how we view people, how we view life and what we do. There are many things that determine who we are. I have listed some areas that I would like for you to identify how they have influenced the person you are today either positively or negatively.

"Search me, Oh God, and know my heart; test me and know my anxious thoughts. See if there is any offensive way in me, and lead me in the way everlasting" ~ Psalms 139:23-24

1. Childhood

_____
_____
_____

2. Words Spoken Into Our Lives

_____
_____
_____

3. Influence of Others

_____
_____
_____
_____

4. Life Experiences

_____

_____

_____

5. Outlook on our Life Experiences

_____

_____

_____

Maybe this is the first time in your life that you have thoroughly searched your thoughts to figure out where things come from. Until you see how you view life, there are no changes that can be made. There are circumstances in your life that are certainly not your fault; however, it is your responsibility to make necessary changes to benefit your relationships. Let's shift our focus on things that can get us off course:

• **People**—There will always be people in our lives who feel as though what they want us to do is what we should do. On that note, we must lay out boundaries so that others do not alter our focus. Stay in tune with God so that, while you may listen to others, it does mean that you must choose their direction. If we are not careful, we tend to say "yes" to things that we are not truly interested in or even gifted at doing.

I was notorious for saying "yes" to everything at the Church and at the kid's schools. I hate to admit it, but I realize now that I took on those responsibilities because I was seeking affirmations and self-worth. I finally had to stop and realize that each time I made a decision based on seeking affirmations, Steve and the kids ultimately paid the price.

What things are you saying "yes" to, that are taking your focus off where it truly needs to be?

_____

_____

_____

• **Commitments**—In order to remain focused, we must have a realistic grasp as to what our commitments are. After God, your very next commitment is your marriage. Many people get that confused with children, church and career. In order for God and marriage to be your top commitments you must stay in tune with those relationships and that takes time. Steve and I got off course here because we poured everything into church. We allowed church and the influences at the church to determine our commitments, which inevitably got us off balance. Bottom line, sometimes we are committed to "good" things when we really need to be committed to "great" things. For example, it has always been a goal of ours for our kids to love God rather than resent Him.

Therefore, we were forced to discern what would best fulfill this goal. For our family, that meant that we were not going to force our children to be at church every time the doors opened because we realized that there were days they did not need church, they needed us. Please understand, places and things of service are good things, sometimes they are even great things, yet they can not replace the input we have in our marriage and children.

What "great" things are you replacing with "good" things?

_____

_____

_____

• **Solutions**—As Christians, we have not learned to turn to God as the ultimate solution. Instead, we look for answers on the internet, in books, through other people and after we have exhausted solutions, it is then that we choose to turn to God. I can remember when we were newly married and in the ministry, we interviewed at a church in Houston. When we left the interview, Steve and I both knew that we were not supposed to accept the job at that particular church. However, my allegiance was still to my Dad. Let's just say I had not gotten the whole leave and cleave concept. So, when we told my Dad that we did not feel as though we were supposed to be at that church, my Dad's response was "you are making a big mistake." Wow, were we torn. Steve was seeking God's discernment and I was seeking my Dad's discernment. It took us a week to battle through this. Here is Steve wanting to pray about this and me never recalling a time when I witnessed my Dad praying over something like this. I believe, however, that this was the moment that I made the choice to follow my husband over following my Dad. It was amazing that we chose to trust and seek God's will and in turn, my Dad ended up affirming the choice we made.

It is not unusual for God to speak to us through people, books or even songs, but if we are not in tune with His wisdom, we are unable to discern what is from Him versus what is from man.

What areas of your life are you and your mate choosing other people's solutions over God's solutions?

_____

_____

_____

• **Desires**—I remember in our early years of marriage that we could hardly be content for desiring what others had. At times, we lost focus in our lives for wanting the kind of house others lived in, the kind of car they drove, the furniture they sat on and the trips they took. If we are not careful, we as Christians can even find ourselves growing a hint of bitterness because of statements such as, "But God I serve you all the time. I give all of myself to you. I give my time, my money, my service and my kind words and here you are blessing others more greatly than me and they don't even live a life that is glorifying to you." Please don't lose the fact that the greatest things in life are not what we can see, but what we invest in. God will bless the desires of our heart as He chooses not as we choose and what we must understand is that there is no conceivable way to fully see what the people we compare ourselves to are going through. Life is seldom authentically represented by what we see on the outside.

Reflection for Direction

A group of alumni, highly established in their careers, got together to visit their old university professor. Conversation soon turned into complaints about stress in work and life. Offering his students coffee, the professor went to the kitchen and returned with a large pot of coffee and an assortment of cups – porcelain, plastic, glass, crystal, some plain looking, some expensive, some exquisite – telling them to help themselves to the coffee. When everyone had a cup of coffee in hand, the professor said: "If you noticed, all the nice looking expensive cups were taken up, leaving behind the plain and cheap ones. While it is normal for you to want only the best for yourselves, that is the source of your problems and stress. Be assured that the cup itself adds no quality to the coffee. In most cases it is just more expensive and in some cases even hides what we drink. What all of you really wanted was coffee, not the cup, but you consciously went for the best cups. Everyone began to eye each other's cups.

Now consider this: Life is the coffee; the jobs, money and position in society are the cups. They are just tools to hold and contain life, and the type of cup we have does not define, nor change the quality of the life we live. Sometimes, by concentrating only on the cup, we fail to enjoy the life God has provided us. God brews the coffee, not the cups...Enjoy what matters in life! Live simply. Love generously. Care deeply. Speak kindly.

Is your focus on life or the cup? Don't be a realist, be honest.

_____

_____

_____

Life Talk

Take heart from Nehemiah, a great man in the Bible. God called him to rebuild the Jerusalem wall. I'm sure there were many times when his focus was tested; however, listen to what happens in Nehemiah Chapter 6. Nehemiah states, "I am doing a great work here, I cannot come down." Four times Nehemiah was distracted by men who were trying to get him to meet them because they were jealous and wanted recognition for the work he was doing. Because of his commitment to stay the course, the wall was built in record time and many benefited. What can we learn from Nehemiah? Are we holding one another accountable and to a higher standard through our friendships and the community God has called us to live in or are we living in comparison of one another causing resentment? Is their an openness to appreciate one another's differences and values so that we grow and learn from each other? It is okay that we live different lives but it states in the Bible that we are called to speak into one another's lives if we see things that are bringing harm or destruction onto others. This is living in true community. Why don't we stop right now, find a partner and speak one minute of encouragement into their lives.

In our marriages, our families, our friendships and our professional lives, we will always have the responsibility of loving, growing and encouraging one another. We must be like Nehemiah, choosing to do the important work and realizing that our choices have the power for others to benefit greatly. Have you realized that the great work God has bestowed upon you is your marriage, family and other relationships?

Choose Life

"Carry each other's burdens and in this way, you will fulfill the law of Christ. If anyone thinks he is something when he is nothing, he deceives himself. Each one should test his own actions. Then he can take pride in himself, without comparing himself to somebody else, for each one should carry his own load." ~ Galatians 6:2-5

CHANCE OR CHOICE?

"When you have to make a choice and don't make it, that is in itself a choice." ~ Williams James

In 1985, Jackie Pflug, a special education teacher at the Cairo American School, was a passenger on Egypt Air Flight #648 going from Athens, Greece to Cairo, Egypt. Three terrorists, calling themselves "The Egypt Revolution," hijacked the flight. A gun battle ensued as the terrorists took control of the flight at an altitude of 35,000 feet. The plane was forced to land in Malta. The terrorists began to execute one passenger every 15 minutes until their demands for fuel were met. Four passengers, one at a time, were executed and kicked down the ramp.

What you must first know before you hear the end of Jackie's story is that the passenger two people in front of Jackie was shot, thrown down the tarmac, began to move and was shot again, moved again and was shot again, and moved one final time to be shot to death. Jackie, who was the fifth passenger, was brought to her knees, shot at point blank range, execution style, thrown from the plane onto the tarmac and left for dead. When Jackie hit the ground she tells the story of something heavy coming over her. And even in her heaviness, she knew not to move, but rather to make the choice to play dead. For five hours Jackie drifted in and out of consciousness until an airport grounds crew retrieved her body, threw her face down onto a gurney and headed to the morgue. On the way to the morgue, one of the medics could no longer look at Jackie's head as a portion of it had been blown off, so he threw her over onto her back and she began to breathe. The medic began to scream, "She's alive, this one's alive." At which point, Jackie says, "are you guys the good guys or the bad guys?" Fifty-nine passengers died during this ordeal. Jackie lived.

While I realize some of you are trying to grab your stomachs back from the visual, I also know that others of you are asking, "What in the world does this have to do with marriage?"

Folks, the one inevitable in this life is death. Jackie Pflug, as she lay on that tarmac for dead, made the choice to live. She made the choice to beat the one inevitable we will all face. And we are simply asking you to make the choice to love your spouse, slow down long enough to play with your children, spend some time with God, laugh, serve and live this one life you have been given. If Jackie Pflug only teaches you one thing let it be to look beyond the obstacles that get in our way and focus our time on what really matters.

Let's talk about some ways we can choose to invest time in our marriage. Let's look at the Three D's:

• **Dialogue Daily**—This is the way we stay connected to our mate. Many times, we believe we are communicating effectively, but in reality much of our communication is small talk and relaying facts. In order to have a heart connection, our daily communication needs to go deeper. What do you mean by that? I'm so glad you asked. First of all, create a safe place where there is comfort, which will naturally take your defenses down. Your first reaction is that you don't have time for this, but please know that if you do not make the time for this, you will be spending a much greater amount of time solving problems when your marriage hits a wall. This is not something where you must spend three hours each day talking. This can be fifteen minutes, thirty minutes or however long it takes the two of you to feel connected. You will know you have succeeded in going deeper with your mate when you can begin to share your opinions with one another, with each partner accepting those opinions rather than dominating them. You will also begin to feel a greater connection when you have the freedom to express your feelings and needs. Walk into this communication heeding the words of James 1:19, "Be quick to listen, slow to speak and slow to become angry." When you do this, ultimately, your heart will soften to the point where you are easily able to share your dreams, your fears and your struggles and hopes with God.

What places do we feel most comfortable and at ease to talk with one another?

_____

_____

_____

Let's evaluate where we both perceive we are in this level of communication.

_____

_____

_____

What are you willing to sacrifice to give each other the time necessary to connect?

_____

_____

_____

• **Date Weekly**—Before marriage, dating was so much fun. Why, then, do many of us give it up after we marry? This does not need to be left to chance, but rather should be a choice that we are going to make time to have fun together. This date does not have to be the stereotypical out to dinner and a movie date. The only thing a date requires is you, your spouse and some creativity. Take turns planning the date. Some ingredients of a great date can include laughter, playing and just concentrating on one another. As a matter of fact, this date can even be free. Go to the park and swing, play putt putt golf, fly a kite, drive to look at houses and dream of the future, walk on the railroad tracks, run through a sprinkler, walk through a college campus and reminisce about the past, skip rocks, hike, fish, workout together, have a picnic, throw a Frisbee, slide down a hill, lay on a trampoline at night and count the stars, drive through the country and find a hidden cafe. You get the idea; just enjoy some fun time with each other ONCE a week.

Let's plan our next date...

_____

_____

_____

• **Depart Quarterly**—How is this remotely possible? Our son has a soccer game, our daughter a cheer competition, the yard needs mowed, funds are low and I can not possibly get everything done at work and you are asking me to depart quarterly. Case in point, there will always be people and things vying for your time and attention. The work will be there when you return, the kids will have other games, the grass isn't going anywhere, but your marriage will have a sense of excitement as you make plans to depart and focus on one another. Do not choose busyness over building long term investments of love. For some of you that are not advocates of leaving your children behind, please understand this may be one of the greatest things you do for your children. When the two of you come back renewed you are more able to give to your children and show them what they all long for, the security of watching a healthy relationship between their Mom and Dad.

What is it going to require for us to depart quarterly?

_____

_____

_____

Reflection for Direction

God demonstrates that He values choice because He created human beings with the capacity to choose. We have the ability to accept or reject his gifts and promises. And while, He may still honor those choices, it does not free us from the consequences of making them. We are responsible for how we choose to live and we will be held accountable by the circumstances resulting from our choices. For many of us, God did not choose our mate, we did, but we are with them now and the choice to honor God and our mate is ours to make.

Randy Pausch, whom many of you remember as the professor from Carnegie Mellon University who wrote <u>The Last Lecture,</u> spoke to Diane Sawyer a few months before he died of pancreatic cancer. The most profound statement I remember hearing him make is this, "Somebody's going to push my family off a cliff soon and I won't be there to catch them and that breaks my heart, but I have some time to sew some nets to cushion the fall and that seems like the best use of my time, so I can curl up in a ball or I can get to work on the nets." The challenge is this; don't wait until it's too late to sew the nets.

Life Talk

We are each given 86,400 seconds a day. How we choose to spend that time is completely our choice. Waste no more time arguing about what a good marriage should be. Have one!

As a group, let's list 10 qualities of a good marriage.

1. _____ **Chance or Choice?**

2. _____ **Chance or Choice?**

3. _____ **Chance or Choice?**

4. _____ **Chance or Choice?**

5. _____ **Chance or Choice?**

6. _____ **Chance or Choice?**

7. _____ **Chance or Choice?**

8. _____ **Chance or Choice?**

9. _____ **Chance or Choice?**

10. _____ **Chance or Choice?**

We challenge you to leave a life of significance rather than success.

Choose Life

"In Him we were also chosen, having been predestined according to the plan of Him who works out everything in conformity with a purpose of His will, in order that we, who were the first to hope in Christ, might be for the praise of His glory." ~ Ephesians 1:11-12

T.I.M.E.

"There is never enough time to do everything, but there is always enough time to do the most important thing." ~ Brian Tracy

Steve and I served at a church for four years in Albuquerque, New Mexico. It was such a great place to live. It was the largest church we ever served at, the salary was awesome, as were the people, the food and the climate. However, it was not a place where our oldest son was thriving. I can remember the day, as though it were yesterday, when we had to begin deciding what was in the best interest of our family for this particular situation. We were initially torn because I'm sure the way Steve felt was the same way most men feel when making decisions that potentially could affect the financial future of your family. The world pushes us to place such security in jobs that we know can support our families. In time, we knew we had no choice but to make the decision that was right for our family and trust God to honor our decision by meeting our financial fears. It was tough. However, what I tell you next taught us one of the most profound lessons we have learned in our marriage. Steve did resign and the day he was moving his things out of his office, his replacement was sitting outside of the door waiting for him to leave. Why do I tell you that? Because you are and will always be replaceable in any job you have. However, you are not and will never be replaceable at home. Your children need you. It seems like just yesterday that our children were small and yet our first grandchild came into the world this past year. You can not get the time you miss back.

As I look back over time, one of the things that grew my love for Steve so much are the days when he would walk through the door early just to be with us. I would say, "Steve, did you finish your work already?"

He would respond by saying, "No, but there are only so many hours in the day to spend time with you and the kids, Ill go back and finish my work after you guys go to bed." Not only did that make me love Steve more, but the relationship that he now has with our grown children is amazing. I even watch our oldest son, who is the only one of our children married with a child and he emulates his Dad in so many ways, especially the way he values his time with his wife and daughter.

What are you giving your children to emulate?

_____

_____

_____

Have you been living a life of success or significance to this point?

_____

_____

_____

While the time you spend with your children will grow them immensely, it will not compare to the time they see you modeling and thriving in your relationship with God. When our oldest son was in high school and playing soccer, Steve and I traveled to an out of town game to watch him play. When the game was over, we went to eat at the same restaurant as the team. Steve and I were at one table and all the players at another. Our son came and sat with us for a bit and while we thought nothing of it, his coach called him to the front of the bus on the way home and said, "Josh, I have been coaching soccer for ten years and I have never seen a player go and sit with his parents while being with the team. As a father of two that really touched me and I was wondering what made you do that?" Josh replied by saying, "When I get up every morning and hear my parents praying for me, it really impacts me and draws me closer to both God and them." Please understand that praying for your children and family does not require getting on your knees every morning and praying some long drawn out prayer. What our children have seen is Steve just coming to where ever I might have been, wrapping his arms around me and praying a simple prayer of protection over the kids and I.

Are your children watching you have a thriving personal relationship with God?

_____

_____

_____

Do you pray protection over your children and your spouse?

_____

_____

_____

Do you trust people enough for your children to trust people?
Do you trust God enough for your children to trust God?

_____

_____

_____

Please understand that while these stories make it sound like we had it all together and just woke up knowing how important time is, we didn't. However, the greatest thing we did for our marriage and family is seek out wise people. If we were around people whose grown children loved each other, we asked how they, as parents, made that happen.   If we were around couples who were balancing time between home and work, we took characteristics they had mastered. There is wisdom all around us, but the choice is ours to reach out and grab it.

Reflection for Direction

Understand that if you do not spend time with your mate and children, someone or something else will. Steve and I have parents ask us constantly, "Why don't my children talk to me about things going on in their lives? Why does it seem they want to be at their friend's houses instead of here?" Our answer always boils down to a question. Have you fostered the kind of environment and relationship that would make them want to spend time at home? If you have not done so, make the time to connect to their world rather than forcing them to connect to your world. Go listen to Harry Chapin's "Cats in the Cradle" song and it will give you a great visual of what happens when you are not spending adequate time with your family.

Life Talk

Let's talk about the difference in quality and quantity time. This is where the little things add up. We have an adopted daughter who runs a camp ministry so we are able to see so clearly a difference in kids whose parents give them quality time and those that seldom take the time to pour value and worth into them. I'm sure if we took the time to look at this, we could also easily see the difference in couples who spend time nurturing their relationship and those that take time for granted, thinking it will never run out. Steve and I absolutely would not trade our quality time for anything in the world. Maybe you are the same or maybe you need help. Let's work together to find some ways to increase the quality of the time we get with those we love. For example, Steve and I will take trips together this coming year, but Steve will also spend time taking our boys on a "guys" trip and me taking our girls on a "girls" trip. This is time that I can guarantee our children will not only give back to their own children, but time they will remember for the rest of their lives. Take the time in your group to discuss great quality time ideas. Discuss ideas that cost little money and those that you make the commitment to save for. Discuss ideas that include your children and ideas that are exclusive for you and your mate.

Choose Life

"Show me, Oh Lord, my life's end and the number of my days; let me know how fleeting is my life. You have made my days a mere handbreadth; the span of my years is as nothing before you. Each man's life is but a breath." ~ Psalms 39:4-5

IRRITABILITY ~ INTIMACY

THE QUESTION I MUST ASK:

**WHAT IS THE ROOT OF MY IRRITABILITY
AND AM I WILLING TO COME FACE TO
FACE WITH THAT ROOT?**

TEMPER TANTRUM

"I lose my temper, but it's all over in a minute," said the student. "So is the hydrogen bomb," I replied. "But think of the damage it produces!" ~ Spencer Tracy

How many of you have a temper? Go with me to the mall at Christmas time. You're a five year old boy or girl walking down the mall with your Mom. You pass the toy store and you say, "Mommy, mommy, I want to go in the toy store." She says, "We are not going in the toy store." To which you respond, "I want to go to the toy store." She says, "We are not going to the toy store, we need to go buy gifts for people we don't even like." You then begin to cry and flop on the floor throwing a temper tantrum. While your Mom should pick you up and adjust your rear end, she instead, gives into you and takes you into the toy store so that your behavior does not embarrass her. At that moment, the bells go ding, ding, ding in your head and you realize, wow, that worked.

Now you are twenty, thirty, forty and you are still acting out what you learned at five. However, it is embarrassing at this age to flop on the floor and throw a temper tantrum so you act it out with a temper. It is acceptable for a child to throw a temper tantrum, but it is ridiculous for a grown man or woman to use actions over words to communicate effectively. In our house, I was the irritable one and I have recently had to hear from my children what it did to them as they were growing up and what it still has the ability to do to them today had I not made the conscious choice to deal with my irritability. Wow, was that a painful realization.

Who is the irritable one in your home and why are you irritable?

_____

_____

_____

How does your irritability make your spouse, family or co-workers feel?

_____

_____

_____

Do you see the same behavioral patterns in any of your children?

_____

_____

_____

Please understand, irritability is not the issue, it is merely a symptom of the issue. It is a lot like having a sinus infection. You can blow your nose over and over again, but the sinus infection is not going to go away without being treated. Irritability is the same way, you can blow your top over and over again, but until you figure out the source of your temper and discontent, nothing in your life will change for the better. Irritability is immaturity of character and if you are subject to being unpleasant and rude to others for no apparent reason, you need to come face to face with the fact that your behavior is extremely selfish. I have come to the realization, because of my own irritability, that for some odd reason we think it is easier to be angry, rather than admitting that we are hurt. So, not only does our own infection get more intense due to a lack of dealing with our hurts and fears, but we also pass our infection onto our spouse, our kids, our friends, our co-workers and anyone else who happens to come in contact with our daily lives.

We have all seen visuals of irritable people. As a matter of fact, we do not even have to look far. Irritable people are all around us. They check us out at the grocery store, they teach our children, they share the office next to us, they answer the phone at the doctor's office, they sit next to us in church pews on Sunday and yes, at times, they even live in our homes. Just yesterday I was driving through Sonic to grab a Diet Coke. The weather was nice outside so I rolled my window down before I ever got close to the drive thru window. I was minding my own business and then I began to hear someone yelling at the top of their lungs. The lady in the car in front of me was screaming at her children in the backseat because they were not giving her their orders fast enough. I mean, come on people, is life that tense that we need to make a public spectacle out of ourselves and even drag our children into it. There is always a better way than flaring your temper to the place of no return. You know the part that is even crazier to me is that when we come into contact with irritable people the first question I am fairly certain many of us ask is, "what did I ever to do them?" Let me help you, you did nothing to them – they have unresolved hurt, fear, anger, bitterness and/or resentment.

When you are in the company of others, do you leave a sweet aroma or a harsh odor?

_____

_____

_____

Let's get personal; when you are in the company of your family, do you leave a sweet aroma or a harsh odor?

_____

_____

_____

Let's take some time to look at 8 characteristics of an irritable person.

If you are the irritable spouse, what characteristics below can you identify are affecting your home or office?

My harsh words: ___agree ___disagree

My lack of peace: ___agree ___disagree

My moodiness: ___agree ___disagree

My short temper: ___agree ___disagree

My controlling nature: ___agree ___disagree

My lack of patience: ___agree ___disagree

My lack of self-control: ___agree ___disagree

My withdrawal from others: ___agree ___disagree

If you are the spouse affected by irritability, what characteristics of your spouse can you identify are affecting your home or office?

His/Her harsh words: ___agree ___disagree

His/Her lack of peace: ___agree ___disagree

His/Her moodiness: ___agree ___disagree

His/Her short temper: ___agree ___disagree

His/Her controlling nature: ___agree ___disagree

His/Her lack of patience: ___agree ___disagree

His/Her lack of self-control: ___agree ___disagree

His/Her withdrawal: ___agree ___disagree

Reflection for Direction

Please understand none of the accountability on this topic is to attack your character or even your irritability, but rather to allow you to see that the time you spend tearing others down or being torn down is stealing a part of your soul. Your soul is your capacity to live, to love, to dream and to have an intimate relationship with God. Once the soul is torn apart, disconnection is imminent. Are you and your spouse soul mates or room mates? If you are room mates you are simply coexisting in the same home and your irritability, temper, passivity and manipulation will never allow you to see the depths of one another's soul. Make the choice today to put your own selfishness aside and become the soul mate that you each desire.

Life Talk

Let's talk, as a group, about whether you are a soul mate or a room mate. Yes, this requires a great amount of vulnerability. Identify first, if you see yourself as a soul mate or a room mate. Next, let's look at the different personality types as that may also help us identify why we do the things we do. Have you ever wondered about how certain people seem to get along and other people seem to clash? Or perhaps you find you clash with certain people and absolutely can not get enough of others. We'll show you a tool that will increase your reliability with people.
While personality types may clash, let's instead find the strengths in each and focus on those:

Personality Studies (Taken from the Four Temperaments Test)

• The **Sanguine** is the **popular person** who wants to have fun out of every situation and be the life of the party. Sanguines love to talk.

• The **Choleric** is the **powerful person** who wants to take control of every situation and make decisions for others. Cholerics love to work.

• The **Melancholy** is the **perfectionist** who wants everything done in order and done properly and who appreciates art and music. Melancholies love to analyze.

• The **Phlegmatic** is the **peaceful person** who wants to stay out of trouble, keep life on an even keel, and get along with everybody. Phlegmatics like to rest.

It is amazing how quickly we can learn to spot these people and therefore know how to approach them correctly.

The **Sanguines** are the easiest to spot because they make grand entrances, love attention, attract people with their magnetism, exude charisma, and tell funny stories. What they want to hear from you is how attractive they are; how you like their hair, look, their new Armani suit, or anything else they have put on to ensure that you notice them. They live for the externals and want you to get excited over their clothes, sense of humor, or new sports car. If you are a Melancholy, you will not naturally be given to praising the obvious and will feel that to laugh at the Sanguine's jokes and stories will only encourage them to babble on.

The **Choleric** Powerful Person is easy to spot because he walks with authority and appears to be in charge of everything. Such people don't want to waste much time on trivial activity with no obvious results or converse with people who have nothing to say of any substance. They are frequently telling other people what to do and pointing out the "dummies" of life. They accomplish more than any of the other personality types, can quickly assess what needs to be done, and are usually right. They don't need to be affirmed on their looks, but they love praise for their accomplishment; their speed in problem solving; their constant goal setting, their loyalty to God, church, parents, business, or country; and their sense of fair play. If you are a Phlegmatic you get worn out just watching these people, but if you want them to be impressed with you, tell them how amazed you are at how much they accomplish in a very short time. They may never have noticed you before but they will suddenly see you as a person of great discernment.

The **Melancholy** Perfect Person is usually very neatly put together and intellectual looking. These people are usually quiet, reserved, and a little ill-at-ease in social situations where they don't know everyone. They would rather talk quietly with one person in depth than banter with a group. They consider compliments on clothes and external niceties to be trivial and want to hear about the inner virtues of integrity, wisdom, and spiritual values. They often marry Sanguines who can't find their way inside these deep virtues and who keep telling them how cute they look. When we don't understand these differences, we are giving out silver boxes that nobody wants. The Melancholy is very sensitive and easily hurt and tends to take what others say in humor as personal and hurtful. Since Sanguines and Cholerics say whatever comes to their minds without weighing their words, they often deflate the Melancholy who is waiting for someone to hand him a silver box that says, "I understand you."

The **Phlegmatic** Peaceful Person is amiable, easy to get along with, and relaxed. These people fit into any situation, blend in with the wallpaper, and modify their personality to get along without conflict. They laugh with those who laugh and cry with those who cry. Everyone loves the low-key nature of the inoffensive Phlegmatic, and though they aren't loud like the Sanguine, they do have a witty sense of humor. They often lean while standing and sit in comfortable recliner chairs if at all possible. They don't need a lot of praise like the Sanguine, nor do they want to be in charge like the Choleric, or get to deeply involved like the Melancholy. They do appreciate being noticed once and a while, being included in conversations that they won't push into on their own, and being told they are of value and their opinion is respected. Since they often marry Cholerics, whose idea of value is wrapped up in how much is accomplished in a given day; they don't get appreciated for their quiet and gentle spirit. They, in turn, find it difficult to praise the constant projects of the Choleric because it wears them out just thinking of them.

What personality are you? Does it enhance or clash with your mate and your peers? Are you willing to understand your mate rather than battle against their differences?

Choose Life

"We who are strong ought to bear with the failings of the weak and not to please ourselves. Each of us should please one another for his good to build him up." ~ Romans 15:1-2

DANCING ON EGGSHELLS

"It is wise to direct your anger towards problems -- not people; to focus your energies on answers -- not excuses."
~ William Arthur Ward

The more I listen and learn from other people's experiences, the more I am amazed at how many people actually believe the phrase, "Sticks and stones may break my bones, but words will never hurt me." Steve and I spend a great deal of time counseling people and I can tell you that we fail to meet someone who has been beaten down with words, that does not either struggle to move past them or pass them on to others. Words are so incredibly powerful and once they have left our lips, there is absolutely no reeling them back in. I've heard some people try to justify, rationalize or make excuses for their harsh words by stating, "You're just too sensitive, don't take things so seriously, this is just how I am." There is a difference between getting angry and being an angry person. When our behavior becomes detrimental to others we are no longer a person with anger, we are an angry person! Please understand, anger in itself is not the problem, but unchecked anger and harsh words can cause paralyzing fear, painful hurt, distance and loss of intimacy with those you are close with. The truth is, harmful and hurtful words can be just as deadly to our heart and spirit as weapons of mass destruction are to our lives.

Do people refer to you as an "out of control" angry person or a person who is respectful and gentle?

_____

_____

_____

Steve recently counseled a man (we are going to call him Tom) who called him on the phone and impatiently said, "Steve, breakfast tomorrow morning, I am so angry I am about to kill my son." Steve met Tom for breakfast and they began talking about why he was so angry. Tom asked his son to take the trash out, so his son picked up the metal trash can, started to the trash bin, and turned to make sure no one was watching him. He then proceeded to take the metal can and scratch his Dad's antique truck all the way down the side. While I'm fairly certain Tom expected Steve to respond by saying, "I would kill him too." Steve instead, responded by saying, "Why do you think your son is so mad at you?" To which Tom stated, "I have no idea, but I'm going to kill him." Steve said, "Maybe you should figure your son's anger out, by first looking at your own anger. Why don't you go home tonight and ask your family if you put them on egg shells?" Ouch!

Do you put your family on eggshells?

_____

_____

_____

That evening, Steve received a phone call from Tom, who again said, "Steve, breakfast tomorrow morning!" Steve met Tom who seemed to have a bit of a broken countenance to him. He sat down and said, "Well, I took your advice and asked my family if I put them on eggshells, to which they all responded yes. They all get tense when I walk in the door. I must admit it was quite difficult to hear." Anger, irritability and harsh words are powerful. They can tear down or build up those closest to us. I don't know Tom's son, but I would venture to guess that the scars left on him by his father's anger, will take time to heal. Tom did decide to leave the scratch on his truck to remind him that he must continually make a conscious choice and commitment to change. Maybe now is a good time to look at your own words and actions.

Have you allowed your words to cut people?

_____

_____

_____

Are you still cutting them? Is it time for a change?

_____

_____

_____

A study by Mary K. Biaggious discovered that both adults and children who were quick to express anger had less self-control, less tolerance and less flexibility than those who were able to keep their anger in check. Children who were slow to anger demonstrated more dependability and social maturity. What I really want you to take the time to look at here is that while you, as an adult, may temper your anger until you are at home where it is safe, this is not the case for a child. Their safety will come at school, in public, at the daycare or at their friend's house. Why do I tell you this? Because some of you have children and you have tried everything you can think of to alter their behavior when what really may need to happen, is for you to alter yours.

Reflection for Direction

This is a hard day of study, but sometimes the hardest topics create the sweetest moments in our lives. It is difficult to see how our actions affect others. However, in your weakness to admit your short comings, you will be loved more and your relationship with God will become much sweeter. I immediately think of a marathon. I have never run a marathon, but I have several friends who have. The first two miles are the hardest, then a rhythm sets in and the run becomes easier, only to feel the burn of the last leg and the exhilaration of finishing the race. Dealing with tough issues in life is no different. The beginning of change will be difficult, then a rhythm will set in and life's issues will seem smoother, only to get difficult again. The question then becomes, will I push through in order to finish well?

Life Talk

Irritability is a huge elephant in the room that we do not want to talk about for fear we may be exposed. And honestly, unless you are extremely passive or the kindest person walking the face of the earth, we are ALL irritable at some point in our lives. While not all sources of irritability are our fault, how we deal with it does become our responsibility and choice. Maybe grief causes your irritability, maybe abuse as a child, maybe the words of your spouse, maybe a narcissistic boss or other things beyond your control. In all of these circumstances, we make one of two choices, we become cynical or we take on an attitude that turns adversity into growth.

When dealing with your irritability, what things make you irritable that are out of your control? How do you deal with your irritability? How do you want others to deal with your irritability? Let's talk about the ramifications of irritability on others.

Choose Life

"The Lord your God is with you, He is mighty to save. He takes great delight in you. He will quiet you with his love, and He will rejoice over you with singing." ~ Zephaniah 3:17

WHAT'S WRONG?

"Spiteful words can hurt your feelings but silence breaks your heart." ~ Author Unknown

Have you ever been in the presence of someone and no matter how hard you tried, you could not gauge where they were or what they were thinking? What an uncomfortable place to be. I can remember one night going over to another couple's house for dinner. They must have been in, how shall we say, conflict prior to our arrival. The husband had obviously pushed through to entertain us; however, the wife put all of us in an uncomfortable position by her silence and the sour look on her face. Let's be real, wouldn't we all have been better off if we would have put the cards on the table, stopped playing games and removed the dad gum elephant from the room. To be real in this situation would have created healing instead of more conflict, because the longer we all sat with the elephant in the room the more uncomfortable Steve and I felt and the larger the conflict was growing between our friends.

Why is it so difficult to deal with what's really wrong?

_____

_____

_____

Some of you have been the victim of a parent's anger and irritability. Therefore, you are merely hanging on to what you have been taught. When I recognized how my irritability was affecting my family, it was pretty late in my oldest son's life. And can I tell you, life isn't fair when you are the oldest child. We have all J's in our family and when I was angry no matter who was at fault, I always yelled at Josh. If you are the oldest in your family, can I just say on behalf of your parents that I am sorry? Because when we have that first child we do not know what we are doing in parenting and we are so afraid that child will be a reflection of our rookie parenting that they better do good and act right. The pressure that we put on that first child is incredible.

We do not realize the effect our happiness or unhappiness has on our children. My irritability was killing our oldest son. He was going through life thinking, "Mom is not happy and it must be my fault." It was not his fault! He just happened to be the one I took it out on. He was safe, if I took it out on Steve he could fight back so I would much rather take it out on Josh. He would look at me with those big eyes and try so hard to make me happy. At the time I realized this, Josh was away at college and God said to me, "Debbie, you have to make that right or Josh will spend the rest of his life feeling like he didn't do things good enough and he kept you unhappy." Wow, did I fight God on that one. As I sat at Jesus' feet one morning, I realized what I had to do the next time Josh came home from school. He came home two weeks later and at half time of a football game, while I had to work myself up to this point; I knew it was time to set him free. I said, "Josh, I need to talk to you, come with me to my bedroom." My heart was racing and I was so scared that he was about to point out to me everything I had ever done wrong as a parent. Josh has always had huge hands and as a baby we would play with his hands and I believe as a result of this, he loves to hold hands. As we were walking down the hall, the sweetest thing happened, he grabbed my hand and in that moment, I felt like God was saying, "Debbie, it's going to be alright, when you do what I have called you to do, I will make it as sweet as it can possibly be." We got back to the bedroom and I said, "Josh, all those years you were growing up, there were so many times I fussed at you and I probably spanked you when you didn't deserve it and I have to tell you I'm sorry and it was not your fault. You were not responsible for my happiness. You did everything you could and I can't let you go through life like this anymore." God's grace is so amazing! With big tears streaming down his face he said, "Mom, it is okay!" The coolest thing is that when I set Josh free, his heart began to soften and turn back to Jesus.

Who do you need to set free from your actions or harsh words so that they can see God?

_____

_____

_____

Is pride, fear or another emotion keeping you from closing the gap between yourself and those you love?

_____

_____

_____

We are not perfect people and we are going to make mistakes. That is life! However, when we choose to deny ownership of our mistakes and fail to make them right we will keep others from seeing Jesus. We are the catalyst for allowing others to see God more clearly. Some of you can not do this for your children or others because no one ever did it for you. I know some of you have been wounded deeply, but can I ask you to see beyond your own pain for the sake of others? Please allow Steve and I to set you free today.

Reflection for Direction

Proverbs 12:18 says, "Reckless words pierce like a sword, but the tongue of the wise brings healing." One of our team building business partners is the professional hockey coach we referred to earlier and I love a story that he tells about the difference in dealing with players in a destructive way versus a way that builds up. He was coaching a player who he depended on for great back checking for his team. When he called the player off the ice he had two choices to make- Choice 1: When the player came off the ice, he could scream at him and beat him down. Hockey players have 45 seconds between shifts. If he beats him down, the player sits on the bench and rocks back and forth with his stick up against his helmet thinking, "I failed, I let the team down." He goes back on the ice and all he can think about is that he has failed and he continues to fail again and again. Or, Choice 2: The player can come off the ice and Scott can say, "John, I need more from you. You are the best back checker on this team. As a matter of fact, you are the best back checker in this league. In order for us to win, we need you to get back." At this time, the player still comes off the ice and while he still rocks back and forth with his stick up against his helmet, he now thinks, "This team depends on me. I am the best back checker on this team. Heck, I am the best back checker in this league." Guess what the player does now when he goes back on the ice? Yes, you guessed it; he busts his tail to get back because he understands that his team needs him.

Same player, same situation, two different choices, but the choices weigh on the decision of the coach. What does this have to do with marriage and your family? Everything! If you beat the family unit down, all you can expect to get in return is failure. However, if you build them up, what you will get in return is unbelievably profound. Reckless words can rip those we have been entrusted with into pieces. Words that build up and are patient, kind, good, gentle and loving create peace. Which is it? Break each other into pieces or build peace in our homes?

Life Talk

As a community of people, you are responsible for holding one another accountable. So, let's have a group discussion to create the openness for communication. Some people are go-with-the-flow cool. Some are easily irritated under certain conditions and others are just plain irritable all the time. How about you? What's your irritability quotient? How quickly do you reach your boiling point? Let's look at some things that can cause irritability.

Are you getting enough sleep?

Do you exercise regularly?

Do you eat a balanced diet?

Do you have financial stresses?

Is pain of the past owning your thoughts?

Is your selfishness causing irritability when you don't get your way?

Choose Life

"Humble yourselves, therefore, under God's mighty hand, that he may lift you up in due time. Cast all your cares on Him, because He cares for you." ~ 1 Peter 5:6-7

INTIMACY WITH PEOPLE

"For a marriage relationship to flourish there must be intimacy. It takes an enormous amount of courage to say to your spouse, "This is me. I'm not proud of it -- in fact, I'm a little embarrassed by it -- but this is who I am." ~ Bill Hybels

Intimacy—in-to-me-you-see! Until we open up our hearts to those we love, we will never experience a communication break through. Before the words flow, our hearts must be exposed. This is not easy. We have to risk vulnerability to the point of possible rejection. It seems that life is so much fuller when we fail spectacularly risking much than to pass along leading a mediocre existence. Wouldn't it be so awesome if we all decided to be a once in a lifetime mate, a once in a lifetime parent, friend, co-worker or servant? We are all longing for people to see us as we are and still love us just the same. We need others and they need us! I think of the words to a George Elliot quote that say, "Oh the comfort, the inexpressible comfort of feeling safe with a person, having to neither weigh thoughts or measure words, but pouring them all out, just as they are, chaff and grain together, certain that a faithful hand will take and sift them, keep what is worth keeping, and with a breath of kindness, blow the rest away." Wouldn't our relationships have such transparency and freedom if we knew that others accepted us just as we are and we accepted them as they are? For this to happen, we must begin by shrinking ourselves so that others stand taller. Steve uses a great illustration. We are both thrown into 10 feet of water and eventually we are both going to drown or I can stand on his shoulders and catch my breath until he taps my foot at which time he can stand on my shoulders and catch his breath. Think of the other alternative, we are in the water and we are fighting each other, the water, the circumstances and our fears. That would not be unusual in such a situation. And actually, the world tells us we are stronger when we can stand alone, on our own two feet. However, intimacy is what pushes us to choose positive results that we can not attain without the other. It is a risk! What if this person does not come down when I tap them for air? Trust is built and commitment becomes strong when someone's actions communicate that I am important enough to save.

Who is lifting you on their shoulders? Who are you lifting on yours?

_____

_____

_____

If you are not, first and foremost, being lifted on your mate's shoulders and them on yours, why?

_____

_____

_____

It is so very important what we do in our relationships. While it is cliché to think that we must trust God so that we can trust others, it is seldom possible that we can trust a God we can not see, feel or touch when the very people we can see, feel and touch continuously dash our spirits. If we are not careful, there are times in our lives that we clutch the past so tightly our arms are unable to reach out and grab a hold of the present. But gosh, while it is so easy to focus on what would hurt if we love and lose, let's focus on what we miss out on if we never venture beyond life's pains into a world where we can see the best in ourselves and others. We would miss out on the joy we have the capacity to experience in our marriages. We would miss out on knowing the very core of our children's souls so that we can watch and cheer on their dreams. We would miss out on laughter, holding onto others through grief and the simplicity of gratitude. We would miss out on the joy of friendships and the diversity each bring to our lives. We would miss out on life's most powerful force – that of loving others and being loved.

Isn't it paradoxical that the very thing we crave so much is what we try and push so far away? We were made to desire love. We were made to crave it, to die for it, to lose sleep over it. We pull people close for it; we push people away when we are scared we have had enough. We will work our lives around it. We will hope for it and hurt for it. We will sacrifice for it. We will criticize and control for it. We will make life changes for it. We are able to go the distance we are not normally conditioned to for it. Why? There is absolutely no force more powerful in the universe than that of feeling loved unconditionally.

When there is an opportunity for intimacy do I push it away or pull it close?

_____

_____

_____

If I push intimacy away, who will be there to pick me up when I fall?

_____

_____

_____

I think Josh Groban says it best in his song, "You Raise Me Up," when he sings the following lyrics, "When I am down and oh my soul so weary, when troubles come and my heart burdens me. I am still and wait here in the silence until you come, and sit a while with me. You raise me up so I can stand on mountains. You raise me up to walk on stormy seas. I am strong when I am on your shoulders. You raise me up to more than I can be." Are you raising anyone up? Are you letting anyone raise you up? Stop living like you don't matter.

Reflection for Direction

Part of intimacy goes with one of the greatest things God gives us—to heal the hurts in our mate that we never caused. Honestly, I think that is the greatest thing one human being does for another—love hurts away we did not cause. When we know our mate has a weakness or a hurt we tend to use that as ammunition, instead of using it to build a bridge of intimacy. When we choose to heal a hurt we didn't cause, we create an arena of safety and unconditional love. I can remember when Steve would do things I didn't like, I would punish him by telling him he was acting like one of his parents. Or when Shelley, our adopted daughter, would put her childhood hurts on me, I would tell her that I was not her biological mother and she didn't need to take her hurts out on me. When the people closest to you act their hurts toward you, it is them simply screaming for you to step back, recognize that it is not personal and love and encourage them through it. This is a concept we don't often hear about, but will you choose to be selfless enough to remove yourself and change a life?

Life Talk

Have you seen the movie *City Slickers*? Go with me to a scene in the movie where Billy Crystal, Daniel Stern and Bruno Kirby are plagued by mid-life crisis and decide to find renewal and purpose on a cattle driving adventure. While herding cattle, they decide to play a game that we will call "Best Day-Worst Day."

Bruno Kirby – *"Look at this, it's a beautiful day. I'm here with my two best friends and we're driving a herd of cattle across the plains. This is one of the best days of my life."*

Daniel Stern – *"OK, what is **the** best day of your life?"*

Billy Crystal - *"You mean, ever?"*

Daniel Stern – *"Yea. Best day ever, in your whole life. And you can't do when your kids were born, that's too easy."*

Billy Crystal – *"I got one. I'm seven years old and my Dad takes me to Yankee stadium. First game and we're going in this long dark tunnel* underneath the stands and I'm holding his hand and we come up out of the tunnel into the light. It's huge, how green the grass was, brown dirt and that grey, green copper roof. Remember. We had a black and white T.V. so this was the first time I ever saw a game in color. I sat through the whole game next to my Dad. He taught me how to keep score. Mickey hit one out. Good day and I still have the program."

Daniel Stern – "Alright, what was the worst day you ever had?"

Billy Crystal – "Worst day. A couple of years ago Barbara finds a lump."

Daniel Stern – "What? You never said anything."

Billy Crystal – "Yea, well it turned out to be nothing. But that whole day was ..."

Bruno Kirby – "Yea, but that was a good day."

Billy Crystal – "How?"

Bruno Kirby – "Because it turned out to be nothing."

Billy Crystal – "Yea, but the whole day until then was hard."

Bruno Kirby – "Yea, but it came out good. You're a real, the glass is half empty kind of a guy. You know that? I don't know how Barbara can stand you."

Daniel Stern – "OK, I got one. My best day."

Bruno Kirby – "This isn't the one about Arlene and that loose step is it?"

Daniel Stern – "No, my wedding day."

Billy Crystal – "What?"

Daniel Stern – "Yea, remember that day. Outdoor wedding, Arlene looked great, those water pills really worked. You guys are all smiling at me and my Dad is in the front. He gives me a little wink. You know, I mean he's not the warmest of men, but he winked. You know, I was the first one of us to get married and get a real job and I remember thinking, I'm grown up. I'm not a goof ball anymore. I made it. I felt like a man. It was the best day of my life."

Bruno Kirby – "What was your worst day?"

Daniel Stern – "Everyday since is a tie." (they all laugh)

Billy Crystal – "Alright, Ed, your best day, what is it?"

Bruno Kirby – "No, I don't want to play."

Billy Crystal – "We did it."

Bruno Kirby – "I don't feel like it."

Billy Crystal – "Okay." (long pause)

Bruno Kirby – "I'm fourteen and my mother and father are fighting again. You know, because she caught him again. This time the girl drove by the house to pick him up. And I finally realized, he wasn't just cheating on my mother, he was cheating on us. So I told him, I said "You're bad to us, we don't love you. I'll take care of my mother and my sister. We don't need you anymore." He made like he was going to hit me and I didn't budge. Then he turned around and he left. He never bothered us again. I took care of my mother and my sister from that day on. That's my best day."

Daniel Stern – "What was your worst day?"

Bruno Kirby – "Same day."

At the conclusion of this scene, the guys get off their horses and play baseball together. You see, being vulnerable with one another allows us the freedom to enjoy one another. Will you play? What is the best day of your life? What is the worst day of your life? Share them with one another.

Choose Life

"Let your conversation be always full of grace, seasoned with salt, so that you may know how to answer everyone." ~ Colossians 4:6

INTIMACY WITH GOD

"What makes humility so desirable is the marvelous thing it does to us; it creates in us a capacity for the closest possible intimacy with God" ~ Monica Baldwin

I used to spend a great amount of time in Dallas buying and reselling jewelry. I would drive three hours to Dallas, purchase jewelry at market and drive three hours back home. Prior to this particular trip, had asked God to highlight the selfishness in my life. Don't ask God to reveal things to you if you don't want to see them. As I was driving down I-35 quickly approaching my exit, I began to pray, "God, please do not give me a red light." You must be thinking, what's wrong with her? There are starving children all over the world and she is using her prayer time to miss the red lights. My reason, however, for praying this is that there seems to be a beggar at every major light in big cities. I know it sounds ugly and selfish, but in being honest with you, I must tell you I don't like them. They are dirty and pitiful looking. So here I am bartering with God, "God, you know I don't like those beggars, so would you please give me a green light?" As I'm writing this, I recognize even more how selfish that sounds and how God must have been going, "Who do you think you are?" But on that particular day, I would be lying to you if I told you I realized even a glimpse of the reality of my selfishness. Come on, I can't be alone in this type of thought process. You know the type of process where we just know God is going to do whatever we ask.

I exited off I-35 and it does not take long for me to know if I am going to get a red light or a green light. Not only did God give me, in His wisdom and sense of humor, a red light, but I am the first car on the inside lane at the light, which means there I am, eye ball to eye ball with the beggar. I am pretty ticked at God at this point and this is what He says to me, "Debbie, I want you to turn around and look at that beggar." And I said, "Not going to do it. You already made me stop here, now you want me to look at him?" To which God replied (not audibly, but in my heart), "Debbie I said for you to look at that beggar." I looked at that beggar in the eyes and it changed my life because I don't think I have ever seen anything hollower in all my life. My look to him seemed to go straight through him and this is what I heard God say, "Debbie, take a look at you, because there you are." I was like, "no, no, no, I think I look a whole lot better than that beggar." To which God replied, "Debbie, you are as empty as that man because you are stubborn, scared and undisciplined and you will not sit with me everyday and let me fill you up. And because you won't, you might as well have a cup because when you do not let me fill you up in the morning, you are a beggar all day long." I have to tell you I experienced a brokenness that day because I realized I was not spending meaningful time with God and all day long I was taking my cup and asking Steve to fill it up and when he didn't, I asked my children to fill me up and when they didn't, I asked my friends to fill me up and if my cup still wasn't full, I asked the world to fill me up. No matter how hard I tried, I could never get enough worth and value from others to fill the cup. I told God that day that I would do what He asked of me, but it scared the living daylights out of me to sit with my Father and allow him to unconditionally love me. I had a father who conditionally loved me and I was so afraid that was how God was going to love me. When I sat down and spent time with God, it was so incredible. He said, "I have been waiting for you and if you will sit here and let me pour incredible worth and value into you, you will no longer be a beggar because your cup will be so full, you will then begin to pour into other people instead of wanting them to pour into you."

What does God need to highlight in your life?
Can you see yourself in the beggar?

_____

_____

_____

Who are you asking to fill your cup each day? If you are allowing God to fill your cup, what are you doing with the overflow?

_____

_____

_____

Is it not awesome, to think of the way God constantly pursues us? He knows us intimately and never loses us in the crowd, doesn't forget us or let us go, even when we may feel otherwise.

Erwin McManus tells a story in his book, Soul Cravings, that is the most profound story I have ever heard about the way God pursues us. He describes a time when he was speaking at a conference in the Middle East and had been invited to speak to a group of Muslims about the history of Christianity. Erwin states, "Pressed by my translator to answer a question that I had somewhat evaded, I was left with no where to go but to talk more specifically and personally about Jesus. I had been describing to them my own sense of disappointment with and even disdain of the religion of Christianity. They all quickly agreed that as a religion, there were deep problems and inconsistencies between beliefs and practices. But eventually they wanted to know what exactly the meaning behind the coming of Jesus was. Somewhat apprehensively I began my best effort to translate back into a Middle Eastern context the story of Jesus and, more specifically, why it would be necessary for God to become human. This, from my vantage point, was the story of God."

McManus goes on to tell the love story of God in this way, " 'I once met a girl named Kim.' My translator looked at me confused. I'm sure he was wracking his brain, trying to remember some biblical character named Kim. He stopped translating and just looked at me. I encouraged him to simply translate. 'I once met a girl named Kim, and I fell in love.' I continued, 'I pursued her with my love and pursued her with my love until I felt my love had captured her heart. So I asked her to be my wife and she said no.' I could feel their empathy, if not their pity. 'I was unrelenting and asked her again, pursuing her with my love, and I pursued her with my love until she said yes.' There was huge relief throughout the entire room. I went on, 'I did not send my brother, nor did I send a friend. For in issues of love, you must go yourself.' This is the story of God: he pursues you with his love and pursues you with his love, and you have perhaps not said yes. And even if you reject his love, he pursues you ever still. It was not enough to send an angel or a prophet or any other, for in issues of love, you must go yourself. And so God has come. This is the story of Jesus, that God has walked among us and he pursues us with his love. He is very familiar with rejection but is undeterred. And He is here even now, still pursuing you with His love."

Wow, if that doesn't make you stand on the table and yell, "woo hoo", I don't know what will. The God of the universe pursues you and me. God is passionate about you and I, and passion produces action.

Reflection for Direction

We recently met with a couple that are trying to make a decision about whether or not to take a job in another city. As we began to talk to them they began to say that they were praying and asking God what to do about the decision. The wife quickly said, "We just don't know if God will show us because we haven't been reading our Bible." Friends, do you understand that God is not like that? He is not sitting up there with a checklist and basing His will for your life or His decision to answer your prayers on that list at the end of the day. I responded by saying, "Whoa, whoa, whoa, all God wants from us is a willingness to hear His answer and then be obedient to it." The problem with many of us is that we are so afraid that God's will for our lives does not line up with our will for our lives. When He speaks to us and we do not listen, we are not only giving up the best for our own lives but we are also standing in the way of what God is trying to do in others through us.

Do you feel that God has a checklist He is keeping on your behalf? What do you think is on it?

_____

_____

_____

Do you feel that God is punishing you for decisions that you have made in your past and that as a result, your life does not deserve the absolute best?

_____

_____

_____

Can you grasp the fact that God is in love with you? Period!!!!

_____

_____

_____

Life Talk

I just love driving to church on Sunday morning watching the people yelling and screaming at each other, swatting at their kids, fighting and being distant. What I am intrigued with is the fact that they get out of their car and are suddenly extremely happy and loving. When you behave this way, you are teaching your children and modeling to your mate that in order for God to love you, you must be happy. Many of you are probably thinking, I do not mind being real; however, how can you remain real with people and not suck the life out of them? Please understand this is about balance. If you are in balance with God and others, you will maintain the kind of relationship where people can accept you for who you are and share their wisdom while not trying to fix you. When you get okay in sharing the vulnerable places of your heart, it also makes others feel as though they are free to heal and be heard and it is then we begin to turn church into a hospital for sinners rather than a hotel for saints.

What kind of environment do you need in order to feel comfortable enough to be real in a setting such as Sunday school, church, a cell group or maybe the family dinner table?

Choose Life

"God is love. Whoever lives in love lives in God, and God in him. In this way, love is made complete among us so that we will have confidence on the Day of Judgment, because in this world we are like Him. There is no fear in love. But perfect love drives out fear."
~ 1 John 4:16b-18

MONEY, MONEY, MONEY

THE QUESTION I MUST ASK:

MY WAY, YOUR WAY OR GOD'S WAY?

WHO WILL I TRUST MOST?

"Living in debt is nerve-wracking, insomnia-producing, and family-wrecking. Just don't do it. There is nothing you can buy that feels as good as being in debt feels bad." ~ Ben Stein

Let us first begin talking about finances by telling you the difference in how Steve and I grew up so that you can see the profound differences that some of us bring to marriage. Steve's family only bought what they absolutely needed and they paid cash for everything. My family bought what they needed and what they wanted and we paid for everything with credit cards. My Mom's favorite hobby was shopping and I was her partner in crime. Every Saturday we would get up and go shopping and she got me to go with her by buying me something. Fast forward now to mine and Steve's first Saturday of marriage.

Steve - *"What are we going to do today?"*
Debbie - *"What do you mean what are we going to do today? We are going shopping."*
Steve - *"For what?"*
Debbie - *"That's not the point, Mom and I went shopping every Saturday."*
Steve - *"What money are we going shopping with?"*
Debbie – *"Don't you have a credit card?"*
Steve – *"No I don't and even if I did, what money are we going to use to pay the credit off with?."*

You see, my Mom used a credit card but she never told me that a bill came at the end of the month that you had to pay. So, I grew up living in lala land and spent a great deal of our marriage loving that place. When Steve told me we were not going shopping I pouted, but I did not get my way, thus initiating our first marital fight.

What did you observe about money growing up?

_____

_____

_____

It is not unusual for couples to be completely opposite when it comes to finances. One partner is typically the saver and the other the spender and while this is not about right or wrong, it is all about balance. If you are out of balance in this area, you will get in over your head. I can assure you, once you get in over your head; it is tough to come back to the surface. Despite money's importance, most of us avoid thinking about our relationship with it. When we do think about money, the topic usually is fraught with negativity and shame, so we keep this relationship tucked in a closet. There are many reasons money is such a hard topic, to name a few: Maybe you did not have money growing up and you do now, so it has become your idol. Maybe you had money growing up and you saw that money was more important than people. Maybe you never have enough, and it has become hard to balance the responsibilities of providing for the same family you are trying to make time for. Just maybe you have too much money and it has distracted you from other important aspects of life. The list could be endless. Bottom line, when there are money issues, no matter what they are, it smothers every aspect of our marriage.

Based on your perception of money, how is it affecting your relationship, positively or negatively?

_____

_____

_____

How do you deal with financial failure?

_____

_____

_____

I can remember so many times in our marriage when I made a bad financial decision for us and because of my fear of failure and my pride, I would approach Steve with such defensiveness. It is so amazing to me that when we begin a dialogue with a fight in us, a fight is exactly what we get back. And yet, I am married to a man who does not identify me by the mistakes I make. When I go to him in brokenness, he is patient, understanding and helpful to find a solution. Why then, do some of us struggle so much to fail brokenly and openly? Please know that I am the pot calling the kettle black when I make this next statement, but maybe we need to just begin and fail and realize that every time we start over we grow stronger.

Reflection for Direction

<u>Ways to Protect/Enhance Your Financial Future:</u>

1. Discuss money before marriage

2. Buy a house you can afford

3. Diversify your investments

4. Choose wise health insurance

5. Don't wrack up credit card debt

6. Don't stay in a dead end job if there are other options

7. Save for retirement

8. Don't ignore credit disputes (Check your credit report often)

9. Create an emergency fund

Life Talk

If we bring such different financial experiences into marriage, how do we determine whose way is the right way? In mine and Steve's case I wanted my way to be right when I wanted to spend money and Steve wanted his way to be right in saving every penny we made. I would say that in this case, neither of us was right and that the answer lied somewhere in the middle. As a Life Group, if we are truly going to live in community then we must hold one another accountable in all things, even the ones we hold so private to our hearts. Find someone in your group that can help guide you and hold you and your spouse accountable in this area if you are struggling to reach a happy medium. Have a healthy discussion about finances in your Life Group. We are often times so caught up in the middle that it is hard for us to even see that we are making unwise financial decisions.

Choose Life

"Keep your lives free from the love of money and be content with what you have, because God has said, never will I leave you; never will I forsake you." ~ Hebrews 13:5

AFFLUENZA

"My idea of being rich — or at least of feeling rich — is to have no debts, mortgage, or overdraft and to be able to pay all bills by return post. This may seem a fairly modest ambition, but if everyone in the West were in this position our societies would indeed merit the term "affluent," and the world would be a much happier place." ~ Paul Johnson

I know many of you are looking at the title wondering, "What in the world is affluenza, I thought this chapter was about money?" I'm so glad you asked. Affluenza is described as a social condition arising from the desire to be wealthier, more successful or to "Keep up with the Joneses." Affluenza is symptomatic of a culture that prides financial success as one of the highest pursuits to be achieved. People said to be affected by affluenza typically find that the very economic success they have been so vigorously chasing ends up leaving them feeling unfulfilled, and wishing for yet more wealth - sometimes addicted to their economic pursuits.

In layman's terms, it means we have become dependent on our checkbooks and the materialism that is arguably present in the United States, where the culture is one that prides itself on possessions and financial success. In other words, we spend money we don't have, on things we don't need, to impress people we don't even like. It is as though we fight so hard to acquire things that are not and will never satisfy our cravings. Please understand that there is absolutely nothing wrong with having money. In fact, there is nothing wrong with having a lot of money. However, when striving to have that money becomes more important than people and/or we acquire much and forget to give, there in is where money becomes the root of evil.

Do you suffer from affluenza?

_____

_____

_____

Steve and I love to refer to Luke 12:13-24 when dealing with this topic. Someone in the crowd said to him, "Teacher, tell my brother to divide the inheritance with me." Jesus replied, "Man, who appointed me a judge or an arbiter between you?" Then he said to them, "Watch out! Be on guard against all kinds of greed; a man's life does not consist in the abundance of his possessions." And he told them this parable: "The ground of a certain rich man produced a good crop. He thought to himself, 'What should I do? I have no place to store my crops.' "Then he said, 'this is what I'll do. I will tear down my barns and build bigger ones, and there I will store all my grain and goods. And I'll say to myself, "You have plenty of good things laid up for many years. Take life easy; eat, drink and be merry." "But God said to him, 'You Fool! This very night your life will be demanded from you. Then who will get what you have prepared for yourself?' "This is how it will be with anyone who stores up things for himself but is not rich toward God." Then Jesus said to his disciples: "Therefore I tell you, do not worry about your life, what you will eat; or about your body, what you will wear. Life is more than food, and the body more than clothes. Consider the ravens: They do not sow or reap, they have no storeroom or barn; yet God feeds them. And how much more valuable you are than the birds!"

When you read that, can you even fathom your worth to our Almighty God?

_____

_____

_____

God takes care of the ravens. Do you even know what a raven is? It is a rat with wings. If God can take care of a rat with wings, wow,

Do you not think he wants to take care of you and me? I have seen God do some things in mine and Steve's married life that still, to this day, blow me away. So, I know that God not only takes care of the birds, He takes care of us, and yet, we still struggle at times with keeping one eye on the Joneses. And I don't mean by the "Joneses" trying to covet what your neighbor has. I am, instead, referring to that thing that society pushes on us to have more, do more, become more.

Steve does not like to shop and he does not like to purchase anything unnecessarily and so when we married he was still wearing clothes that were way out of date. I would always tell my Mom, at every occasion buy clothes for Steve – birthdays, Christmas, Ground Hog Day, St. Patrick 's Day – anything you can think of, he just needs clothes. I fell in love with Steve's heart, not the way he looked on the outside. Anyway, we had been married a few years and I told him that we needed to go and get him some clothes for work. Of course, it took me two weeks to prime him for this because he didn't think he needed anything. On the Saturday we were going to go, I got dressed and came into the living room where Steve was waiting on me. He was sitting on the couch and I said, "Let's go." To which he responded, "Come sit down by me." When I was growing up my Dad would say, "Debbie, get your checkbook and come sit down," which usually included a lecture about money. So, when Steve asked me to sit down, I thought, here we go again. I came to the couch in defensive mode, but I sat down and Steve said, "We are going to pray." I said, "Pray for what, we're not about to eat." He just looked at me like, Bless her sweet heart and said the most basic prayer, "God, you know our needs and you know how much money we have and I'm asking you to show us where to go."

When Steve finished, I thought, this is a new one. I have been shopping my entire life and I have never prayed about it. Of course Steve thinks I prayed with one eye open saying, "Jesus, don't let us forget the credit card." We arrived at the mall and began walking past stores. I see a men's store and say, "Let's go in here." And he said, "I don't think that's where we are supposed to go." I honestly could not

73

figure out what was going on, my mother and I went in every store in the mall. We continued to walk and as I saw the next men's store I said again, "Let's go in here." He said, "I don't think that's where we are supposed to go either." I am getting irritable at this point. We get to the third store and I'm thinking, "Surely, we can go in this one" and he said, "No." I really got ugly at this point. I go "Ooh, did the spirit not move you?" He just ignored my ugliness and stayed the course. We finally got to the end of the mall and the last store is Dillards and Steve says, "Yes, we can go in here." I say, "Hallelujah, we get to go into a store." We went into Dillards and made our way to the men's department and begin going through the sale racks. We are ministers; we have no money at this point in our marriage. We began flipping through the racks minding our own business and this gentleman wearing a Dillards name badge that read Rick McAfee, walked over to us, put his hand out and said to Steve, "You're Steve Wilson. I know what you do and I appreciate you." Steve said, "Well, thanks!" To which Rick asked, "What are you looking for?" Steve said, "Some slacks and sport coats for work." Rick said, "Come over here with me." I'm looking at Steve because I know that "coming over here with me" is more than we can afford. Pride grabbed us at this point, so instead of saying anything to Rick, we followed him over to the "expensive" section, but we are looking at each other the entire time not sure what to do or say. Rick is not paying attention to us, he just begins pulling out things in Steve's size and Steve finally says, "Rick, we really appreciate you trying to help us, but I have to be honest, we can not afford these things." Rick responded by saying, "Steve, I know. I am the buyer for the men's department and because I appreciate what you do, as long as I'm here, I'm going to give you clothes at cost." I quickly said, "Is there a women's store?" We were there three years and anytime we needed something Rick gave it to us at 75% off. Why do we tell you that story? Because many of you are so dependent on your own ability to manage your finances, you don't pray about anything dealing with your finances, you just go buy. And Jesus wants you to depend on Him because He can show up even in your purchases at the mall.

Do you only pray about the big things in your life?

_____

_____

_____

**Do you believe that God's faithfulness extends from the
monumental things in your life to the trivial things?**

_____

_____

_____

Have you ever tried praying for every need?

_____

_____

_____

No one ever taught me or demonstrated to me that every need is important to God. I spent most of my life short changing God because He wanted to meet us at our need and yet, my lack of patience seldom waited on Him. Let's not get confused here; there is a difference in asking God to meet our needs versus asking Him to give us the desires of our hearts. And while, God may come through on both, He may also make us wait on both in order to build character and maturity, while also developing a greater dependence on Him. God absolutely delights in our dependence on Him.

Steve and I had been married just a couple of years and it was Monday-you guessed it- wash day! I went to the laundry room to begin washing only to realize that I had no soap. I went to my checkbook and saw that I only had a couple of dollars and payday was still two days away. Remember, I was the irritable one in our home, so you can imagine the tone of voice I used when Steve happened to call me. It's amazing to me as his timing has always been impeccable.

My sweet husband always finds a way to put a positive spin on situations so he said, "Debbie, just forget the wash today. Get Josh dressed, make a picnic lunch and go to the park." I was not particularly happy about it, but I got Josh dressed, slapped the peanut butter on the sandwiches and got together what we needed for the park. I opened the door to leave and as I stepped out, I tripped over a box of Tide. I was scared to touch it, I didn't know if it dropped from the sky or if Steve had called the benevolence committee. I walked to the end of the driveway and looked down the street and there was a white truck putting new and improved Tide on every doorstep. What we realized years later is that God knew we had a need long before we knew we had a need. That company was scheduled to deliver that Tide on our street weeks before we even knew that would be a need.

Do you struggle believing that God can meet your needs? Why?

_____

_____

_____

Reflection for Direction

Steve and I stepped out on faith eighteen months ago to do fulltime marriage ministry. It was not, initially, an easy transition. We went from having a fulltime salary and benefits to walking completely by faith. I am certain that we were able to take the leap of faith because of the dependency we placed in God for the little things. Have you even stopped to reflect on the areas of God's faithfulness in your own life? Too many times we tend to take credit for the good things that happen in our lives, only leaving God room to solve things that we are uncertain we can attain alone. Your faithfulness in the small things will allow God to be able to trust you with bigger possibilities. I think as parents, we want so badly for our children to have faith in God, even during times when we are not even certain we have faith. I am certain that as a result of our diligent faithfulness even amidst the scary times, that not only have we been able to spread God's word, but two of our children have also stepped out on faith to lead community ministries

Life Talk

While this may surprise some of you, money is the primary competitor with God for our time and affection. Many of us will even unconsciously allow God every aspect of our lives, and yet never surrender our finances, believing we can manage them far better than God. Ellen Goodman wrote, "Normal is getting dressed in clothes that you buy for work, driving through traffic in a car that you are still paying for, in order to get to the job that you need so you can pay for the clothes, car, and the house that you leave empty all day in order to afford to live in it." She also goes on to say that the average American spends more than $21,000 a year on consumer goods. To emphasize her point, Goodman notes that each week Americans spend six hours shopping and only 40 minutes playing with their children. Yes, society has created this all around us, just like society has not helped in so many other choices we make as human beings but it is our responsibility to rise above what society has created to the place that God has called each of us to. This life is not about who has more, how they got their money or what they are doing with their money. It is about how we sacrificially give at our "own level" instead of competing and that, my friends, is the prescription for affluenza.

Too many times, when it comes to our financial distress we allow our pride to keep us from admitting that we are struggling. What would our small community look like if we were all able to push our pride aside and admit things such as: We don't have it all together; We have mismanaged finances; We have an abundance of money but spend frivolously; We want to do good things with our finances but no one has ever taught us how to manage money. I challenge you to figure out ways to get real, yes even in the private matter of finances. I am not talking about spreading your bank statements around the room, but I am talking about growing in wisdom together and using this time to create an open discussion about finances.

Choose Life

"The disciples were amazed at His words. But Jesus said again, children, how hard it is to enter the kingdom of God! It is easier for a camel to go through the eye of a needle than for a rich man to enter the kingdom of God." Mark 10:24-25

IT COST WHAT?

"There are plenty of ways to get ahead. The first is so basic I'm almost embarrassed to say it: spend less than you earn."
~ Paul Clitheroe

Have you ever really stopped to think about what things cost? Sure, it's easy to figure out that we want the $1.19 brand peanut butter over the $1.47 brand. Seldom, however, do we spend the time to think about what that $25,000 car really is going to cost us long term. Or how much that $300,000 home is going to cost over the next thirty years. And yet, we sit at the table many months with the same worries, fears and problems. Too much debt, too little money and an uncertainty of what the future holds financially. Jesus knew that money would be an issue for us, so much so, that over half of the parables he wrote dealt with money and the Bible contains over 2,000 verses about money. We are crazy if we think he did not want us to "get" it. 90% of people in our culture buy things they can't afford and I would venture to guess that an even higher percent are in denial about their true financial status. Ok, some of you are going, this chapter has nothing to do with me, my spouse and I have an abundance of money or my mate and I seldom ever purchase something we can not afford. While I recognize that each of you reading this, sit at different places in your life, the reality is that money is the central core of our being. It is an issue that we will all deal with at some point. As we write this, our economy is in terrible shape, so even if you have an abundance of money, you are probably stressing about your net worth. And there will always be future expenses to worry about. How much will it cost to send your children to college? How will the next house note be paid? How will we buy our child a car at sixteen? What kind of retirement do we have? What if an emergency medical trauma happens?

The dialogue about money is never ending.

What future concerns do you have financially?

_____

_____

_____

What are you doing today to deal with those concerns?

_____

_____

_____

Do you communicate as a family about money?

_____

_____

_____

Realize that to whatever level you communicate as a couple about money, is how your children will view money. They will develop either balanced qualities about money, frivolous spending or responsible saving. You are the key to this.

I once read a quote that said, "The easiest way to teach children the value of money is to borrow from them." That quote makes me laugh because I think of one of the pro hockey players that work at our camp in the off season. He and his wife and kids were driving in Dallas through the toll booth, only to realize they didn't have any cash to pay the toll. Quade turned to the backseat and said to his son, "Ben, can I borrow the dollar bill that you have?" To which Ben replied, "No, Dad that's my money." Quade then responded with, "Ben, if you give me that dollar, I'll pay you back two dollars." Ben said, "Make it three and it's a deal." Ben is seven and even at seven a child can and will understand the value of money if he is taught. How, then do we begin to teach children about money at an early age? A great place to begin is by reminding your children that allowance is not an entitlement but rather a tool for teaching the importance of saving, budgeting and giving. A good way to teach your children how to manage money is to do the "envelope" system. As a family you can each have three envelopes, one for spending, one for saving and one for giving. This will allow your children to actually see the visual of what is happening with their money as kids do not realize what things cost.

Have you taken the time to sit your children down and talk about the value of money?

_____

_____

_____

Steve spent many years as a youth pastor and I can remember one year at youth camp, we were asked to teach a "financial" class to a group of high school students. We both thought, this should be interesting, what can we possibly teach kids about the management of finances? Wow, was that a wakeup call to the naivety that many kids have about money. We began by asking them to help us put together what they perceived their family budget to be. Let's look at the difference in a teen's perceived monthly budget of the average four person family versus the real budget of the average four person family.

	Perceived cost by teens	True cost
House note ($250,000 home)	$480	$1576
Utilities	$90	$400
Car Note ($25,000 car)	$250	$460
Car Insurance (2 cars)	$50	$400

Groceries (per month)	$200	$600
Health Insurance	$150	$1000
Total Monthly	$1220	$4436

The list could be three pages long and could include things such as taxes, entertainment, clothing, credit card monthly statements or school tuition. You get the point—today's generation of young people do not understand what it cost to run a household and as a result, many are unprepared to enter adulthood at the end of high school or college. Finances are a private matter and we are not asking you to tell your kids about your every financial move and bill. We are simply encouraging you to help your children understand about debt, about saving, about giving and about the cost to live a simple lifestyle versus one where they buy whatever their heart desires. 80% of college students have credit card debt before they even graduate from college. 80%! That means that 8 out of every 10 college students will begin their career "in the hole." I am beginning to believe that every college in the United States should have a mandatory financial class that each student must attend before graduation.

Let's talk about patience. Do you teach your children, or yourselves for that matter, how to wait on things that maybe God is not ready for you to have or that you can not afford?

Do you trust God's discernment and faithfulness to choose what is best for you in the area of finances?

Steve was serving at a church in Albuquerque, NM in the early 90's. Albuquerque had a gated golf community called Tanoan that we would constantly drive by from our house to the church. Without fail, every time we would drive by the subdivision our youngest son, Jordan, would say, "I want to live in Tanoan with the little man at the gate." Jordan thought if we lived there absolutely no harm would come to us because of that little man, however, we always responded, "Jordan we are not going to live in Tanoan." The homes in Tanoan ranged anywhere from $500,000 to $2,000,000. Steve and I knew that living in Tanoan was not something that we were capable of making happen for us, but we had a choice: we could tell Jordan to stop talking about living in Tanoan and explain to him that the houses in Tanoan were too expensive for Steve and I or allow this as a teaching ground for Jordan to realize that sometimes we want things and even though we ask God for them, He teaches us that He will choose what is good for us to have and maybe not so good for us to have. So, each time we would drive by the Tanoan community and Jordan would repeat, "I wanna live in Tanoan," we would say, "Jordan, pray about it." Every night that child prayed, "Jesus, I wanna live in Tanoan with the little man at the gate so he can protect us."

What we came to realize was that Jordan did not want to live in Tanoan because he was intrigued with the size of the houses. He was always our insecure child and he thought that if he lived in that subdivision, the little man at the gate would protect him. This went on and on from November to May. May rolled around and Steve and I attended Janae's graduation from kindergarten. Before the ceremony began, one of Janae's classmates' parents came to Steve and said, "After the ceremony, may we please speak with you as we have a proposal that we would like the two of you to discuss." Scott Ruska was one of the members of the team that invented the Intel micro chip and he was so intelligent that I can not do justice to the intellectual accent he possessed when he approached Steve. I can remember asking Steve what Scott had said to him and Steve responded by saying, "I'm not sure. I think he has something he wants to talk to us about after cookies and punch." The ceremony finished and we sat down in the little preschool chairs with our punch and cookies and the conversation with Scott and Paula went something like this: "Steve and Debbie, I work for Intel and they are sending me to Ireland for fifteen months. Paula and I have been talking and praying and wondered if you would consider living in our house for fifteen months?" We were renting a house at the time because our house in Tyler had not yet sold. Guess where Scott and Paula lived? Yes, you guessed it, Tanoan. Scott said, "Now, I know you're a praying man and need to pray about this." To which Steve responded, "You know, there are some things you just don't need to bother God about."

We left the kindergarten program and we were in tears because, to us, it was the fact that we would have no house payment for fifteen months, which amounted to over $15,000. However, to Jordan, it would mean that God cared about his security. And both of those overwhelm me still to this day. We were always in the process of teaching our children how much God loved them, so we devised a plan. While we wanted to run home and tell this to the kids, we thought this would be a great tool to have Jordan continue to pray since we were not going to move into the Tanoan house until January. Every night, Jordan continued to pray. We even found ourselves pouring gas on the fire by saying, "Jordan, are you praying about Tanoan? Pray, pray, pray." Jordan would say, "Daddy, I'm praying." Steve would respond by saying, "Pray harder."

Each year at Christmas, we have a tradition of a "family" gift. We would have one present that we would open last and the kids could hardly wait to open it. This particular year, God revealed to us that the family gift would be to announce to the kids that we were moving to Tanoan. We wrote a note and put it in a box and then in a bigger box and still a bigger one and then wrapped it. Steve asked Jordan to open the family gift. Jordan began opening and he would shake the present and say, "There's nothing in here." We would say, "Keep opening." He finally got to the note, which said, "Jordan, what have you been praying for?" He screams, "Tanoan." The note continues, "Jordan, because of your faithfulness in praying, we are moving to Tanoan in January."

84

Am I saying that if you teach your children about money and then have them pray to live in a multi-million dollar golf resort that God is going to move you into one? Absolutely not! I believe that Steve and I set out to do something good for our family by getting out of debt and I believe that God turned our good to great because of our discipline. But, even more than that, I believe that God looked down into the condition of Jordan's heart and the perseverance with which he prayed and listened to the faithfulness of a child and granted him the desires of his heart.

Those life changing experiences have made an impact on our lives and our children's lives that will never disappear. It is an amazing scar that we will constantly remember. God has continuously said to Steve and I, "I do not want you bound by anything because for you to be bound by debt or by conflict or by selfishness or by stress you are not going to be your full potential for me. I am going to teach you a lesson or two along the way so hold on for the ride." God is so good to discipline us because he loves us and because of obedience and a willingness to be disciplined, he will bless the socks off of you every single time because if you know the same God we know, then you know there is always hope.

Reflection for Direction

I would not trade the Tanoan lessons for anything in this world; however, I did not like that house. I could not find any of my family and I realized that I'm probably never going to have a desire again to live in a house of that magnitude. But what that house will always represent to me is the fact that when we, as a family, make the conscientious choice to handle money the way God wants us to, He will bless us over and over and over again. Elizabeth Warren says, "Paying for yesterday is perhaps the most important investment you can make in your future. Getting rid of those debts will buy you breathing room. It will buy a future of freedom. And it will bring your dreams — the things you really, really want — into reach." Decide to live a life where you not only teach your children how to manage their own finances, but also one in which you can dream and fulfill the life God has called you to live. There are enough people working jobs for money and wouldn't the world be a happier place if some were working jobs because they loved them.

Life Talk

The question isn't what do you own? But rather what owns you? Spend some time in your group discussing this thought. How can you help each other with budgets? How can you help each other in teaching your children how to budget and understand money? What stresses do you have from buying so much and yet, spending such little time with your families? Are you overworking to buy something that will never satisfy you?

Choose Life

"A faithful man will be richly blessed, but one eager to get rich will not go unpunished." Proverbs 28:20

TO LIVE IS TO GIVE

"You have never truly lived until you have done something for someone that can never repay you." ~ Author Unknown

I am not sure that there is anything more gratifying in this world than giving back some of what we are taking out of it. Giving just makes the soul feel cleansed, refreshed and anew. I think of various things Steve and I have given in this life, whether it were our tithes, helping someone out in need, donating to a non-profit, serving the homeless or simply walking by and picking up someone's ticket to pay in a restaurant. Can I just tell you, I don't ever remember missing that money? Please know, I am not telling you that to toot our horns, we have simply given back what so many others have given to us. I just think it's crazy. We seem to feel the hurt of the money that we spend on meaningless ventures or objects, but it has never ever hurt us to give something away. Winston Churchill says, "We make a living by what we get, we make a life by what we give." Wow, is that ever true? You don't have to give money; give your time, give your words of encouragement, give your heart, give your talents and your abilities. You do not have to give to a hundred either; just give to one and you will experience God's divine love in a new way. And as Steve and I have so clearly learned, sometimes God will prompt us to trust Him and give and other times he will use someone else to bless us unexpectedly.

Has God asked you to unexpectedly give? Did you? If not, why? If so, how did it make you feel?

_____

_____

_____

"Religion that God our Father accepts as pure and faultless is this; to look after orphans and widows in their distress and to keep oneself from being polluted by the world." ~ James 1:27

When was the last time you and your family looked after the orphans and the widows? If you have never, you are missing out on one of the most incredible things this side of heaven.

_____

_____

_____

Are you your own charity or have you allowed others to be your charity?

_____

_____

_____

One of the most enriching things we have been a part of as a family, is serving another family. Our previous Director of Cleaning at our family camp is not only raising her teenage daughter, but also her two grandchildren as their mother (her oldest daughter) passed away several years ago of diabetic shock. We were so inspired by Ms. Nancy's commitment to willingly take her grandchildren in and love and provide for them as her own, that we desired, as a family, to be closer to them. It really began as the adoption of a family for Christmas. We showed up on Christmas Eve to their home bearing gifts, with our oldest son dressed as Santa Claus. We came with bicycles, video games, Nike shoes, money and other things to give them the kind of holiday season that, we too, were blessed to have. I remember at one point, one of our children said, "We are not here as a charity case. We are here because you guys have blessed our family and taught us about the commitment to love one another in times of crisis." So, not only did we show up, we played and enjoyed one another's company with no separation lines of race and socioeconomic status. As a gift to us, Ms. Nancy's oldest son played Silent Night on the saxophone and in that moment, I know we were all ushered into the presence of a great God.

One of things we have learned about giving is that the one time wonder is easy. It's continuing to make an impact that is tough. We have, however, continued our Christmas giving with the Butler family for the past four years. This past year at Thanksgiving, our oldest daughter received a call from Ms. Nancy and she was crying. She proceeded to tell Shelley that she and her children were living in a shotgun house in a neighborhood where they could smell marijuana seeping through the doors of their duplex apartment. Steve and I were at dinner that night when Shelley called us and was panicking and we knew God was calling us to get Ms. Nancy out of that house. As we continue this story, please hear our hearts, we are not telling it to toot our horn. We are simply trying to give you a look as to some areas where we have given as a family and, as a result, God has blessed us greater than we ever deserved.

We were able to find Ms. Nancy and her children an apartment in a safe neighborhood and we were so excited that we decided to do this "Home Makeover" style. Our family and our camp staff sent Ms. Nancy to work and we moved all that was worth keeping from her old house and were able to get new beds and new furniture donated. We then went and purchased new towels, bed linens, vibrant pictures and furniture. When the house was complete, we called Ms. Nancy and she and her children came home to the first safe home they have ever had. As Ms. Nancy walked through the house she wept, we wept, her children wept and the feeling was nothing short of winning $100,000. It was incredible. The icing on the cake, however, was when Ms. Nancy called that night and asked if we had an air mattress she could sleep on. We asked, "Why do you need an air mattress, you have a brand new bed with clean linens." To which she responded, "I have never had a new bed and I have certainly never had new linens, most less ones that matched the bed spread and I am afraid that if I sleep on them, I might mess them up." Can you imagine? While you and I are sleeping on matching linens and have never even given thought to it, there are others who see matching bed linens as a miracle only God could provide to their lives.

The next morning we received another phone call from Ms. Nancy and this time she was weeping. We could barely understand what she was saying, but finally this is what we heard, "I wanted to thank you guys for what you did. Since my daughter died, I have never been able to hang a picture of her on the wall and this morning when I woke up, I saw the picture you had hung. I was able to healthily begin grieving her for the first time. On the other side of my wall, I noticed you hung a mirror; something else I have never been able to do is look at myself in the mirror. I do not want to need help in this life and I have always felt that because I do that I am a failure to my children and grandchildren. Because of what your family has given, I was able to look in the mirror this morning and say, 'Why don't I deserve this?' I believe that God loves me and what an incredible time to begin teaching my children about God's unconditional love and blessings."

Oh my goodness! To think that had our family not been willing to give a small portion of what God has so willingly given us, what two families would have missed out on. We, as a family, would have truly missed out on what it is like to be ushered into the presence of a great and almighty God. And the Butler family would have not only missed out on the safety of their living environment, but also the grieving of a deceased child and the amazing goodness of God's grace and mercy. Giving is not about you! It is about what God created us for and has called us to.

What, my friends, is keeping you from giving?

_____

_____

_____

Do you think you don't have enough? You might not, but God does.

_____

_____

_____

Do you understand that by not giving, you are missing out on something tremendous? "Give and it will be given to you. A good measure pressed down, shaken together and running over, will be poured into your lap. For with the measure you use, it will be measured to you." ~ Luke 6:38.

Reflection for Direction

Don't allow yourself to be your own charity. Sure, you have to pay your bills and in order to retire; you even need to make a monthly contribution to things like your 401(k) or your Roth IRAs. But find something else meaningful to give to. The amount of your gift or even your time does not matter. Five dollars may seem insignificant to you; that is not the case for the single mother who finds herself in a position far, far more troubling than yours. Consider the areas in which you are fortunate. If you are reading this book, you have some measure of literacy and intelligence. You have access to instant communication and all the opportunities that go with it. You have comprehension and potential for growth, as well as, access to technology and the benefits it can provide. You and I are immensely fortunate.

Consider all the instances in your own life in which events might have gone abruptly against you, but didn't. Somehow you emerged unscathed, or God may have made you better by unexpected experiences. Let us now consider the opposite. What if things had happened in your life and you were not able to push through? Where could you be now? If something does go wrong, what will your reality be tomorrow morning? Whatever problems, fears or pain you can imagine, know that someone is there right now. And if we, as Christians, do not help them, who can we count on that will?

As cliché' as it might sound, there is no way of describing the feeling you receive from giving freely of yourself, and doing it with zero strings attached. Let's change the way we bless others with our time and money as wealth is not about what we can buy, or the amount of the money we have in our account. It is, instead, generosity.

Life Talk

As a small group, come up with a project that can bless someone else. When the project is completed, answer the following questions together.

How did the experience make you feel?

Would you consider doing it again?

Who was more blessed? You or the person you gave to?

Choose Life

"A gift opens the way for the giver and ushers him in the presence of the great." ~ Proverbs 18:16

BLESSINGS

"Blessed are those who give without remembering and take without forgetting." ~ Elizabeth Bibesco

The definition of blessed is highly favored or fortunate. For many people highly favored might mean being liked by the boss and co-workers, maybe fortunate could mean having all that we want and need. But for some reason, I can not get my mind off the fact that blessed has nothing to do with what I have and everything to do with the fact that my relationship with God makes me highly favored and fortunate. And yes, that is difficult to wrap my mind around.

Can you remember ways that God has unexpectedly blessed you?

_____

_____

_____

It seems that everywhere Steve and I have served; people give us their old used car. This does not faze Steve as he is grateful for anything and is just not real caught up in what he drives as long as it gets him from here to there. When we were in Albuquerque, Steve was driving a run down Datsun 280zx. One morning our pastor asked Steve if he could give him a ride to the hospital to visit someone, as his car was in the shop. The car had a standard transmission and the clutch was going out so you could not let it out fast, you had to ease it out and give it a little gas and whoa, there it is. It finally grabs a hold of you and you get whip lash. Steve took the pastor to the hospital and when they were returning to the church, the pastor got out of the car he said to Steve, "Remind me to never ride with you again, that car is dangerous."

Steve said, "We have two cars falling apart so pray for us."

Steve had a meeting with the Associate Pastor at the church at 11:00am on Friday morning and he asked him to pray for us. He told him we had two cars falling apart but that we had committed to get out of debt and because of that we did not want to go into further debt by purchasing a new car. The pastor said, "Yea, but we have dealers in the church and I know someone will give you a good deal." Steve said, "I know, but we made this commitment and we just want to pray it through." The two of them prayed and when they finished Steve said, "Man, we need to hurry and get to the golf course." They were playing in an FCA golf tournament and their tee off time was 1:00. Steve asked Jesus in his heart at an FCA camp in Estes Park, Colorado when he was eighteen and because of that he really has a fondness for FCA. Playing in this golf tournament has always been a way for him to give some money back to the organization to send kids to camp where he asked Jesus in his heart.

The guys teed off at 1:00 and they started on the 7th hole and played the 8th and 9th. Steve was playing horrible, hitting the ball out of bounds. There was a tornado warning, which never happens in Albuquerque because the Sandia Mountains break down the tornadoes. The wind was blowing that particular afternoon at 30 mph. We lived in Albuquerque for five years and it was the only day we remember having tornado warnings. The guys teed off at the 10th hole; a par five, Steve hit the ball out of bounds again and decided to just leave it. You have to understand, Steve is the guy who hits his ball into the woods just so he can go and find the balls left by others. Steve made his way to the 11th hole, a par three, one hundred and fifty yards to the hole with a little lake in front of the hole and 30 mph winds from right to left. The gentleman in front of him stepped up and hit into the sand trap to the right. Steve got up to tee off and started praying, "Jesus, let me keep this ball in play. I don't have any balls left in my bag and I really like this one." Steve hit the ball to the right and oh, I forgot to tell you, on this hole if you hit a hole in one, you win a car. Steve hit the ball and it went off to the right where it went out of bounds. Remember the 30 mph wind; it carries the ball to the

95

left and drops it 20 feet from the hole. The ball rolled 19 feet and 11 inches and stopped. One bigger gush of wind comes and clink! The guys all begin screaming, "It's in the hole! It's in the hole!" Steve won a $17,500 car.

It is unbelievable what God does with our money when we make the decisions He would have us make. The story does not end here. Steve shared with the congregation at our church about us praying to get out of debt and him winning the car. A dealer from the church called him the next day and asked him what the taxes were going to be on the new car. Steve proceeded to tell him that they would be about $2,500 and the dealer told him to bring his Datsun to the dealership and he would buy his old car. Steve drove the Datsun to the dealership, which he says looked like a Flintstones movie with the car sputtering and smoking and him just praying that it would make it to the dealership. He walked in and took the title to the dealer and the dealer handed him an envelope. Steve walked outside and opened the envelope to find that there was $2,500 in the envelope to pay for taxes. He walked back inside and told the dealer that there was no way the Datsun was worth $2,500. To which the dealer responded, "I can make that car worth whatever I want it to be worth. I do not want that free car to cost you any money." That particular year, when we decided to get out of debt, God gave us a car, a house to live in for fifteen months and an anonymous deposit in our bank account for $5,000.

Reflection for Direction

Our fallacy is that we tend to define blessings as something big. Are you able to take your next breath? Do you have food? Are your children clothed? Can you worship freely in your country? Do you have some semblance of roof over your head? Then you, my friends are blessed. We told you a story about God giving us a car, but more than that, God has provided for our every need on a daily basis much more than the big things. Maybe the key is that we need to have gratitude for the little things and realize that it might not be what we want, but God gives us everything we need. This is all a matter of perspective and your perspective IS your reality. We are no different than the Israelites. They constantly lost sight of God's provisions for them and every time they lost sight, they turned away from God. Hello Christians, when we lose sight of the daily blessings we will walk away from God as well and worship other idols.

Life Talk

After spending the last week studying money, blessings and giving, your heart must surely be open to the blessings in your own life. Have you each stopped to applaud God in this area or are you still taking the credit? Take time to do an inventory of your life and "count your many blessings, name them one by one, there's no greater way to have a heart of gratitude."

Choose Life

"Praise the Lord. Blessed is the man who fears the Lord, who finds great delight in his commands." Psalms 112:1

DRIFTING

THE QUESTION I MUST ASK:

WILL I GO WITH THE CURRENT OR

AGAINST THE CURRENT?

WHERE DID WE GO?

"Every day you spend drifting away from your marriage is a waste not only of that day, but also of the additional days it takes to regain lost ground." ~ Author Unknown

We absolutely love the beach in our family. We love it so much that when we go out for the day it looks like we are moving. We take our chairs, umbrellas, ice chest, floats, towels, food and beach games. And yes, we usually make Steve carry it all. We bunker in and get our little area ready for a day of sun and surf. And while there are many things we love about the beach, our favorite thing to do as a family is to hop on our floats, paddle past the tide, link our rafts to one another and just talk and play. After an hour we will look toward the beach and inevitably one of us will say, "Someone moved our stuff." We all know that no one moved our stuff. Instead the current slowly moved us down the beach. That is a picture of marriage. We have our wedding day, we get our little nest settled and before we know it the circumstances of life have caused us to move from the starting point and to drift away from one another.

Can you identify?

_____

_____

Spending time together was so fun when we were dating and newly married and then maybe we stopped communicating and there became an awkward distance between us. Maybe the day to day hustle and bustle of life left us too tired to connect. Regardless of where you got lost, we have to recognize that communication is the connection between two people. We must make an honest connection everyday if we are going to stay in tune with one another's feelings, emotions and needs. Steve and I began to recognize at the twelve year mark that we had drifted apart. Our kids were young and there just didn't seem to be the time for each other between church, homework, ball games, careers, school functions and the daily routines that zapped us of our energy. Looking back now, I am certain that had our communication stayed in tact, we would not have hit the major wall that we did not even recognize was moving in on us.

Let's take a minute to evaluate where your communication level with one another is:

■ **Non-Existent**

■ **Small Talk**

■ **Anger and Frustration**

■ **Honesty With Freedom To Share Feelings**

Isaiah 43:18-19 says, "Forget the former things; do not dwell on the past. See I am doing a new thing. Now it springs up; you do not perceive it. I am making a way in the desert and streams in the wasteland." God does not want you to put your marriage on cruise control, He instead wants you to choose this day and this time to recognize where you have drifted apart and to press on to all He has in store for your marriage. Please understand, drifting is normal and from time to time it will happen in our marriages. But we must not accept the drift, we must recognize it and persevere through it, not giving up and not giving in. While it may begin to sound repetitive in this book, the pursuit of marriage must be intentional. When the current begins to pull you under you must not let go of each other, but rather ride the storms out. If you default to the values of our culture, you will pursue the large house, the great body, the successful kids, the addictions, the emotional connections with other people and your marriage will drift.

Are you willing to accept your role and responsibility in the drifting of your marriage or are you still believing that someone else is responsible for "moving your stuff?"

_____

_____

_____

Is your marriage valuable enough to you for you to begin to understand your mate rather than seeking to be understood?

_____

_____

_____

You see there can and will be multiple reasons your marriage has drifted apart, but it will not come back together if you do not begin to accept your role in the process. Our daughter recently printed some statistics off the internet to share with the community in order to grab community awareness on such things as single parent homes, childhood obesity rates and low self-esteem in children and the numbers were alarmingly devastating. 2.1 million Children in the United States are now living in single parent homes. 50% of children suffer from the pain of divorce. 1 in every 3 children suffers from low self-esteem. Why do I bring these statistics out during drifting? Because folks, if we do not get serious about pulling things back together as a couple, our decisions will affect a generation for many years to come. As a matter of fact, some of you are drifting because of the unfairness done to you as a child and it is in this time that we must take responsibility and create a cycle of change. Our children are now grown and thriving in their lives, but I am only a memory away from realizing that had we not made the choice to honor our commitment to one another, their lives could have most certainly taken a different path. Will you please be vulnerable enough with each other to restore your marriage to a healing place?

Reflection for Direction

Drifting is such a subtle, unconscious thing that happens. Marriage is tough! Somewhere between "We are gathered here today" and "Til death do us part" there is a lot of real life going on—ups and downs, highlights and failures, dreams attained and dreams lost. Real-life marriage is hard, a balancing act of jobs, children, friends, in-laws, paying bills, cooking meals and maintaining a home. Not only these, but we also deal with transitions to different stages of marriage— adjusting as newlyweds, working dual careers, having kids, kids growing up, moving, changing jobs, and growing older. Often the one we're supposed to love most is lost in the confusion of life. You need to put activities into your life together to help you to enjoy and encourage each other as husband and wife as well as to foster talking, learning and growing together.

Life Talk

We recently did a marriage conference and after the conference a couple emailed us and simply said, "Thanks for helping us take a trip back to the beach, we didn't realize we had even drifted." Will you take a trip back to the beach with us? What are 3 things you loved the most about your mate when you fell in love? What are the 3 things you love about your mate as a parent? What are 3 things you love about what your mate gives to your home? What are 3 things you love about your mate and their relationship with God? What are 3 things you love about your mate around your friends? What are 3 things you love about what your mate provides to your home?

Choose Life

"See to it that no one misses the grace of God and that no bitter root grows up to cause trouble and defile many." ~ Hebrews 12:15

IS THIS AS GOOD AS IT GETS?

"Love is not written on paper, for paper can be erased. Nor is it etched on stone, for stone can be broken. But it is inscribed on a heart and there it shall remain forever." ~ Author unknown

"If this is as good as it gets, I'm not sure I want to stay." That, my friends, was my quote to Steve at the twelve year mark. I don't know that I can even tell you everything I felt or that I had even pen pointed all that was wrong. I just knew that this was not the life I signed up for and I was out! I laugh now because Steve and I have been married for over thirty years and I could not love him more and had I left that day without us working so hard to figure things out, I don't want to even fathom who we would both be today. Steve jokes all the time, "If you ever leave me, I'm going with you." And while I get tickled with that statement, I also love the fact that I know he is not going anywhere and I am not going anywhere. We have allowed God to create in us a strand that can not be broken.

Every marriage will hit a wall between four and ten years and we will be forced to ask ourselves, "Will we coast or push through the wall?" When we hit this wall we can choose from three options.

Option A

Hit the wall and say we are in this for life.

Option B

Hit the wall and talk about divorce. And please hear me, if divorce is an option you will NEVER work on Option A.

Option C (This is where most Christians live)

Hit the wall, back up to the point of least resistance and then coast. If you decide to coast, you will last for a little while but eventually someone will get dissatisfied and walk away. Or you will become a bitter old person.

We've all seen bitter old people. In our family, we call them "Luby's" people. Go with me to your local cafeteria between 4:45pm and 5:30pm. An older couple stands in line with their tray. She gets her food, then he gets his and she says, "Why are you eating that, you know its not good for your diabetes and cholesterol level?" To which he responds, "I think I'll have two." They get their food and sit down and don't speak for the 25 minutes it takes them to eat. Finally, they are done and he says, "You have money?" She says, "I thought you had money." He says, "You know I don't have money, you never give me any money." They finally pay the bill and head home to sit in their recliners for the 6:00 news and another episode of Matlock. What a miserable existence. But, do you know when a bitter old person became bitter? They became bitter between the ages of 25 and 40 years old when they chose not to deal with their issues. Let's take a look at one of the issues—unmet expectations.

What expectations did you bring into the marriage?

_____

_____

_____

We all brought a set of expectations to our marriage. Very rarely, however, were those expectations discussed. My mother read me fairy tales growing up, but failed to tell me they were not true. As a result, every time I saw a movie or something romantic in the world, that is exactly what I expected my future marriage to be. I wanted the "knight in shining armor riding up on his white horse, swooping me up into a romantic kingdom" experience. Wrong!!! Steve does not have a romantic bone in his body or a white horse and every time I anticipated or thought he would or should be romantic, I was totally disappointed. Steve, on the other hand, assumed that I would cut lettuce for his salad like his mother did and that Betty Crocker here would also have sex all the time with no reservations.

Unmet expectations will *always* lead to disappointment. This is a never ending theme of our lives. Steve does not struggle with unmet expectations like I tend to. For example, if he calls me during the middle of the day and says that he will be home early and he is not, it has the ability to color my night. If we are not careful, those little disappointments will build up over time to the point of wanting to walk away. How then do we deal with these unmet expectations? We enter marriage with a picture of what it should look like, yet we marry an imperfect partner. We therefore have a choice:

We can keep the picture and tear up the person

OR

We can keep the person and tear up the picture

In your marriage have you made the conscious decision to keep the person or the picture?

_____

_____

_____

If we are not careful we can waste years trying to make our mate to fit into the picture. Choose today to tear up the picture and cherish the amazing person God has joined you with.

Reflection for Direction

We have all, at some point in our lives, asked the question, "Is this as good as it gets?" Maybe you, like us, have asked it in your marriage. Maybe you have asked it in your family, with your friends or in your career. Bottom line, if you are unwilling to admit that it has at some point been a thought in your mind, you are in serious denial. The good news, however, is that there is hope once we come face to face with changing our perspective on how we will accept our unmet expectations. We hear from couples constantly that have lived for years drifting apart from one another and never noticing until a crisis hits or until it is too late. I read this quote recently, "Regardless of weather, the moon shines the same; it is the **drifting** clouds that make it seem different on different nights." Marriage is no different. The person you married twenty years ago is the same person, but the trials, the circumstances, the financial stresses, having a difficult or sick child, the death of a loved one or unmet expectations has made you believe differently.

Life Talk

Let's discuss as a group how much we have bought into unrealistic expectations for our life. Can we ever just admit to each other that sometimes life just stinks, that sometimes we are disappointed and that at other times we just don't have any answers? We come before our peers and we want to have it all together thinking that will somehow impress our friends and make them love, admire and respect us more. That is a crock! They love, admire and respect us more when we are able to admit and take responsibility for our fair share of our drifting and the way we feel about life's disappointments. What disappointments have you experienced that have caused you to drift? (i.e. Finances, In-laws, Health, Tragedies, etc.)

Choose Life

"When times are good, be happy; but when times are bad, consider; God has made the one as well as the other. Therefore, a man can not discover anything about his future." ~ Ecclesiastes 7:14

MARRIAGE IS A COVENANT

"Every man who truly loves a woman, and every woman who truly loves a man, hopes and dreams that their companionship will last forever. But marriage is a covenant sealed by authority. If that authority is of the state alone, it will endure only while the state has jurisdiction, and that jurisdiction ends with death. But add to the authority of the state the power of the endowment given by Him who overcame death, and that companionship will endure beyond life if the parties to the marriage live worthy of the promise." ~ Gordon Hinckley

On a website called Craig's List, a young woman wrote: "I'm a spectacularly beautiful 25-year-old girl. I'm articulate and classy. I'm looking to marry a guy who makes at least half a million a year. Where do you single rich men hang out?" She also wanted to know how men decided between "Marriage versus just a girlfriend. I am looking for MARRIAGE ONLY," she said.

In response, a man who claimed to meet her financial requirements said that from his perspective, her offer was a lousy business deal. "What you suggest is a simple trade: you bring your looks to the party, and I bring my money," he wrote. "But here's the rub: Your looks will fade and my money will continue to grow." "So in economic terms you are a depreciating asset and I am an earning asset." (Ouch!) This is why, the man explained, "It doesn't make good business sense to 'buy you' (which is what you're asking), so I'd rather lease. So a deal that makes sense to me is dating, not marriage. If you want to enter into some sort of lease agreement," he finished up, "let me know."

Well that was pretty harsh! Now plenty of readers thought she deserved it. She was turning marriage into an economic transaction —

reducing what would be a sacred relationship into nothing more than a contract—and that's a dangerous mistake.

I did not marry Steve as an economic transaction, but in reality is that much different than marrying someone because we are asking them to complete us? Immediately I think of the movie, *Jerry Maguire* when Tom Cruise said to Renee Zellweger, "You complete me!" No human being can complete me or you or anyone else for that matter. Only God can do that. 1 John 4:12 says, "No one has ever seen God, but if we love one another, God lives in us and his love is made complete in us."

Why did you marry?

_____

_____

_____

While you may have married what was *your* choice for a mate, the day you said "I do" you entered into God's choice and what should be a covenant for life.

All throughout the Bible, God made covenant with his people. He told them to trust Him. He would be the strongest partner they would ever have and their only responsibility was to obey His word. God never wrote the rules or the specifications on paper for his people to sign; instead He gave the promise from a heart of love and care for his children. The world, on the other hand, says, "Trust no one! Protect yourself."

Are you protecting your marriage or yourself?

_____

_____

_____

It is almost impossible to protect both because if you are thinking of yourself first, you are not giving adequate protection to your marriage. Economist Jennifer Roback Morse, author of the book <u>Love and Economics</u>, puts it well. When it comes to marriage, she says, "The language of contract is misleading because it undermines the basis of generosity and self-giving that is so important in married life." Morse is right. Contractual arrangements are a calculated effort to get what you want on the best terms you can get it. But marriage is about unreserved giving and sharing. Contracts are limited and renewable; marriage is a permanent, life-long commitment. It is about self-sacrifice, not self-satisfaction.

The Scriptures back this up. Ephesians 5:28-30 says, "In this same way, husbands ought to love their wives as their own bodies. He who loves his wife, loves himself. After all, no one ever hated his own body, but he feeds and cares for it just as Christ does the church-for we are members of his body." Christians have always seen marriage as a covenant with God. Couples are to put aside their own selfish desires and focus on the needs of the loved one. But the values of the marketplace, applied to marriage, teach a totally different message: that is, that we are entitled to a good "return on our investment." They turn would-be brides and grooms into marital consumers, looking for the best deal they can get. Tragically, people who think this way often end up in a kind of unholy wedlock—one in which men abandon wives the moment their looks begin to fade, and women drop their husbands if they run out of money.

In your marriage, have you agreed to a contract or are you living out a covenant?

_____

_____

_____

Huh, you ask? What's the difference? I just signed whatever they gave me to sign at the Church the day of the wedding. Let me see if I can clear up the confusion.

The difference between a covenant and a contract marriage may look like this:

Covenant	Contract
Loyalty	Loop Holes
Way Through	Way Out
Faith	Skepticism
Selfless	Selfish

Let's start with one of the greatest qualities you can have—loyalty. I remember a time when Steve came home with our first dog. This dog was the most pathetic looking thing I had ever seen. He was obviously a stray, as he was eaten up with ticks and fleas and had lost patches of hair. One of Steve's greatest qualities is that he has always seen the potential in worn down things. I knew his compassion would not let him walk away from that dog. He bought flea and tick shampoo and gave that dog quite the scrubbing. When he was finished, he began to pull every tick, one by one, off that dog. The dog would whimper and wince and Steve would say to him, "Trust me, you're going to feel better when we finish." When the bath was finished and all the ticks had been removed, that dog lay on the floor and was probably free of pain for the first time. What does this story have to do with a covenant marriage? That dog only had eyes for Steve. Everywhere Steve went, the dog went. The dog was grateful toward his master. What an amazing picture of God and his covenant. He loves us and is so loyal to us, yet we forget to be loyal back at times even though he has taken our hurts, fears, burdens and sins and placed them upon His own shoulders.

A covenant marriage should look the same; both mates, taking one another's burdens, fears, dreams, hopes and emotions and remaining loyal enough to hold them with such care and tenderness assuring the other that all will be okay.

Are you a loyal person?
Are you loyal to your mate first and foremost?

_____

_____

_____

Does your mate ever have to wonder if you will seek a way out?

_____

_____

_____

Have you cherished your mate's dreams and hopes? Have you helped them heal from their wounds, scars and fears?

_____

_____

_____

We live in a contract weary society, in which most men are worried about taking care of themselves first and therefore, a contract assists in assuring that will happen. And while I do not think there is anything wrong with a contract, as a matter of fact, they are necessary in today's times, a marriage can not be built on a contract because there is always a hidden clause that will allow you to get out. It may be costly to you, but it is not impossible.

A covenant, on the other hand, is an agreement made in trust between God and another person. God sets the terms and makes the offer, we then decide to accept or reject His offer. When we accept the offer we 'make' the covenant. In a covenant, the parties put no limits on their responsibility. Bruce Hafen explains it so well in his book, Covenant Hearts. He states,"The difference is in the attitude of contract versus the attitude of covenant. In contract both parties are hoping to limit liability or maximize profit or otherwise make things better for themselves. The contract is then a way of ensuring that things go just as planned and, if necessary, to force the other party to promised action. This is the shepherd who was *hired* to watch the sheep. He'll do it as long as he gets paid and as long as there's no danger to himself. A covenant relationship is one in which certain terms are set, yes, but the parties make the cause of the other their own cause. In other words, when I make a covenant, the goals and desires of the person with whom I am covenanting become my own. Conversely my goals and needs and desires become the goals and needs and desires of the One with whom I am covenanting. This is the lesson of the good shepherd. Christ makes the life of the sheep as important to Him as His own life. What a blessing it is to be able to make covenants with God. When we fulfill our side of this 'two-way promise' He is able to apply his infinite power and wisdom to our tiny problems and trials. Even death is overcome by his power. This is a contract so overwhelmingly in our favor that we would be foolish to reject it."

Reflection for Direction

It first occurred to me that our marriage might be in trouble when my wife won an all expense paid trip for two to Hawaii - and she went twice. I couldn't help but read that statement and laugh, but if you think about it, that is probably how so many couples live today. He does his thing, she does her thing and they simply co-exist in the same home. Better yet, this marriage is so represented by a contract that when one of you does not measure up to the look you married for, you're done! When one of you trusts your parents to solve your problems more than your mate, you bail! When the financial means are not what you had initially dreamed them to be, you run! When raising children or step-children became harder than you thought, you quit! When you wanted to have children by the age of thirty and it didn't happen, you disconnected! You see, in a covenant all of those things still happen, yet there is no quit, there is no running, there is no disconnect, instead you allow them to pull you together and draw you closer to God. The visual that immediately comes to mind is that of Field Day. Do you remember the three-legged race? You tied yourself to your partner and you were not going to break the chain for anything. You crawled, you sprinted, you fell, you held on for dear life, whatever it took to get to the finish line. A marriage covenant should be much the same way.

Life Talk

Now you are probably thinking, that all sounds great, but here we are at a crossroads right after our miscarriage, we can't control the decisions of my ex-husband in order to deal better with the step-children, my wife's depression isn't going away, if we don't take the job in the other city it is going to stall our financial freedom for the future and so on. As cliché as it sounds, I love the quote, "that which doesn't kill you makes you stronger." That is so true and we will believe it for an athletic contest, or we will push it on our children when it comes to studying, but when are we going to believe it for our marriages? So what do we do to hang on tightly to each other through the trials? First of all, you must begin giving each other the freedom to express feelings. Secondly, you must stop blaming each other for the pains of life. It is absolutely natural to pull away from each other in tough times because none of us want to feel bad things. Do you pray together? Do you pray for each other? Will you make the commit and accountability in your community group to first pray together for your own marriage and then to pray for each other's marriages?

Choose Life

"Oh Lord, God of Israel, there is no God like you in heaven above or on earth below-you who keep your covenant of love with your servants who continue whole heartedly in your way." ~ 1 Kings 8:23

PERSERVERANCE

"Perseverance is the hard work you do after you get tired of doing the hard work you already did." ~ Newt Gingrich

Life is tough! We all have to work through difficulties and life without them is impossible. The world will tell us there are ways to ease our troubles, but in reality the world's ways are a mere numbing tool. James 1:2 says, "Consider it pure joy, my brothers, whenever you face trials of many kinds, because you know that the testing of your faith develops perseverance. Perseverance must finish its work so that you may be mature and complete, not lacking anything." It puzzles me that it is even remotely possible to be mature enough not to be lacking anything.

As we write this book, I will admit that perseverance is not something easy for Steve and I to turn our focus toward. I have never, in my life, had to persevere through anything as difficult. As a matter of fact, when we began writing our adopted daughter asked me, "Mom, have you ever played on a team?" I said, "What do you mean have I ever played on a team and what does that have to do with writing a book?" She went on to say, "When you have been on a team, you realize that when you are tired and want to quit, you can't. You see, the team is counting on you and if you quit, not only do you let others down, but you also put the team in jeopardy." Ouch! I guess I never stopped to think about it.

Did you ever play a team sport?

_____

_____

_____

Do you know how to be a team player?

_____

_____

_____

Do you realize that your marriage and family are YOUR team?

_____

_____

_____

The answer is no, I have never played on a sports team, but I can remember having to make the choice to be on the "Wilson team." You see, when Steve and I hit the wall at the twelve year mark, we shut life down, we packed up the kids and we headed to the beach. The beach became our training field and our family became the team. In order for us to begin shaping our goals and hopes for the future, we had to first begin by figuring out what we had done well in our marriage to this point and where we had failed. It was not easy hammering away at the adversity and there were times I wanted to quit, but then we would look out at our children and know that if we quit, we were going to teach them also to quit. And quitting, my friends, is a scary thing. The first time you do it, it's the hardest thing you will ever do, but eventually it becomes easier and easier as trouble comes. It pains us still today to think what that would have done to our children.

For one week we sat on that beach and we made the choice to train as hard as we possibly could, in order to create the goals of a marital championship. There were times it hurt and times when we would get the break through we needed to keep us pushing through. When it got tough, we had to push harder and when we saw a little light, we rejoiced in the hope of restoration.

When, in each of your lives, have you persevered through to the point of pain in order for your marriage and family to be better?

_____

_____

_____

If you have never pushed through, what are you waiting on?

_____

_____

_____

I can remember that life began to look a little brighter each day that passed on that beach. And honestly, it always does when we persevere. We may start the day feeling as though there is no hope but eventually a peep of sunshine will come through the clouds, giving us enough hope to wait for tomorrow. And at some point, the tomorrow of our marriage became sunnier with each passing day. Maybe your need for perseverance does not come from your marriage hitting a wall. Maybe it comes from the loss of a parent, a child, or another loved one. Maybe it comes from a past of mistakes that you can't allow yourself to move beyond. Whatever, the case, it is not an option to give in. It is an option, however, to embrace a life of change and set on a course for your marriage that may look different than the one the world has set. History is full of examples:

The first steamboat took 32 hours to go from New York City to Albany, New York. _People laughed._

A horse and buggy passed an early model car. _People laughed._

The first electric light bulb was so dim they had to use a gas lamp to supplement it. _People laughed._

The first flight lasted 59 seconds. _People laughed_

And as you choose to put your commitment to marriage at the forefront of your life, _people may laugh._

Failure is inevitable or perseverance would not be necessary. And honestly, we may fail many times but we are not and will not be a failure until we make excuses as to why we failed. I can't help but think of a baseball player. He can fail 70% of the time and still be an All-Star. That is only 30% success rate and he becomes one of the greatest players to ever play the game. Why can't marriage be like that? Why can't we go through life recognizing that we are not going to hit it every time we swing? Let's decide today to focus on the great things each of us brings to the marriage and not the weaknesses.

Reflection for Direction

I once read a quote that said, "I fall, I get up, I fall again, I get up and all the while I keep dancing." What a phenomenal picture of marriage. I am going to fall! You are going to fall! It is inevitable. Think about when your children started playing sports at a young age, one of the children on the team would fall down and the kids would all stop playing to help the child up. We, as parents, would all be screaming, "Play, get the ball, keep running." Then our children turned fifteen and someone would go down and the kids would keep playing and we, as parents, were all screaming, "Stop the game, someone's down." Marriage is so much like that. When we are newly married, oh we will stop life and make sure our mate is good, but then ten, fifteen or twenty years go by and life is so fast paced that we leave our mate behind.

Life Talk

Ephesians 1:5 says "Husbands, love your wives, just as Christ loved the church and gave himself up for her to make her Holy, cleansing her by the washing with water through the Word, and to present her to himself as a radiant church, without stain or wrinkle or any other blemish, but Holy and blameless." Christ sacrificed everything for us— everything! Therefore, how we can leave our mate behind? We have allowed ourselves to forget what Christ did for us by buying into "women's lib", "you are all you can count on", "make more money", "step on anyone who gets in your way of success", "God can't do it, you must do it yourself." As a result of forgetting what Christ did for us, we are unable to completely sacrifice ourselves for a healthy and whole relationship with our mate. Paul makes it clear that a marriage should be a precious relationship that needs tender, self-sacrificing care. How should a man love his wife?

1. He should be willing to sacrifice **everything** for her.
2. He should make her well-bring of primary importance.
3. He should care for her as he cares for his own body.

Do you understand that no wife will ever fear submitting to a man that treats her that way? What sacrifices are you making for your marriage? Do you even know what sacrifice looks like? I know, with absolutely no doubt in my mind that Steve would lay down his life for me. How do I know? It began with little things. He would sacrifice golf so that he could be with the kids and I. He would sacrifice going to the movie he wanted to see for the one I wanted to see. He sacrificed time to follow behind my car at night to make sure I got to my destination safe. When the cable man came, he ran home so that I would not be home alone. I realize those things sound simple on the heels of what Christ did for us, but it is the little things that will ultimately lead to the great sacrifices.

Choose Life

"The Lord himself goes before you and will be with you; he will never leave you nor forsake you. Do not be afraid; do not be discouraged."
~ *Deuteronomy 31:8*

HE WHO BEGAN A GOOD WORK

"To have and to hold from this day forward, for better or worse, for richer for poorer, in sickness and in health, to love and to cherish to death do us part."

"Being confident on this day, that he who began a good work in you will carry it on to completion until the day of Christ." ~ Philippians 1:6

As Steve and I sat on that beach in Gulf Shores, Alabama, I was not sure that what God had begun would be seen to completion. It was so hard to pull out all the hurt, neglect and raw feelings. Just when I was ready to say "forget it", I looked over and saw our oldest son, Josh, watching us. I honestly do not know what he was thinking, but I do know God used that look to show me how much our children NEEDED us to make things work. If we fell apart, they would fall apart as well. As parents, Steve and I would do anything and everything for our children. On the shore of that beach, we had to choose to work through all the difficulties and pain so that we could have a great marriage and our children could have the security they so desperately needed. Maybe you are that couple or even more so, maybe you have been taken back to the day when you were that child whose parents made choices that are affecting your own marriage today.

God is so good. Good enough that he whispered Philippians 1:6 to us for the remainder of the week. The day Steve and I married, God began a good work and He was crying out to us not to ruin what He began. He just kept pushing us to attempt to realize that if we would just hold onto Him and our commitment to one another, He would be faithful to finish it and finish it far better than we could imagine or dream.

Are you going to give God a chance to finish what He began?

_____

_____

_____

If you will give God the chance, He will continuously find ways to remind you of His great faithfulness. Do you remember when Joshua was about to take the Israelites across the Jordan River into the Promised Land? In Joshua, chapter 4, God told Joshua to choose twelve men from among the people, one from each tribe, and take twelve stones from the middle of the Jordan to the place where they would stay that night. Joshua obeyed God and his people laid the twelve stones. In Joshua 4:24 it says, "He did this so that all the people of the earth might know that the hand of the Lord is powerful." I believe God wanted his people to have a reminder of His faithfulness to them. I believe we also are to have stones in our own lives to remind us of all God has done for us personally.

God gave us such a tremendous reminder while we were at the beach of the stones in our lives. Steve and I married on July 15, 1978. On the Sunday evening of our honeymoon, we attended First Baptist Church, Houston. It was a very large church and Steve and I slipped in quietly and sat at the back of the church. At the welcome, people came and introduced themselves to us and welcomed us to the church. We happened to mention to one of the couples that we were newlyweds and were in the ministry in Missouri. Everyone sat down and what happened next could have only come from God. John Bisagno, the Pastor, stood up behind the pulpit and told the congregation of a couple attending that night who were married the night before and serving in the ministry. Yes, you guessed it; the couple he was speaking of was Steve and I. He asked if we would come to the front so that they could pray for us. I will remember that day for the rest of my life as though it were just yesterday. That pastor, who seemed larger than life at the time, put his big arms around us and prayed that God would bless us and use us mightily for His kingdom. Wow, I can hardly write that without weeping tears of gratefulness. On that day, God began a good work in us and while we could not the see the future, nor could we see the profoundness of that day, in that moment, God did see the future. And He knew that a day would come when we would be forced to choose between remembering how we hurt each other; the day, the week and the year before or remembering, instead, where the start of the journey began. On that day, God laid the first of many stones and He was intent on us remembering it. He was going to be faithful to us, but were we going to be faithful to Him?

Do you fathom the concept that on the day you said, "I do", what an incredibly awesome work God began in you?

_____

_____

_____

What was the first stone God laid for you?

_____

_____

_____

Reflection for Direction

It may be difficult for some of you to journey backwards. There may be hurts that you are unwilling to feel the painful memories of once again. Trust has been broken and you are uncertain that you can ever trust again. Our passionate hope is that you will at least go back and give it all you have. If you do not give it a shot for yourself and your mate, please at least battle for your children. Steve and I know that we are seeing the hard work of perseverance come alive in our children. One of our sons is married, but our other three are in dating mode. We see in those three how much they seek the approval of Steve and I. I don't believe they are seeking approval because they want us to ultimately choose their mate or because they are trying to please us, instead I believe they are seeking the kind of approval from us that we have learned only through the wisdom attained in battling through our own hard times. They, without saying it, are asking for accountability in laying their lives down for another human being the way they have watched Steve and I do so for one another. Are you willing to go to the place in 1 Corinthians 13 where "Love is patient, Love is kind, It does not envy, it does not boast, It is not proud, It is not rude, It is not self-seeking, It is not easily angered, It keeps no record of wrongs. Love does not delight in evil, but rejoices with the truth. Love always protects, always trusts, always hopes, always perseveres. Love bears all things, believes all things, hopes all things, endures all things. Love never fails?"

Life Talk

In writing the notes on this particular life talk, we happened to also be proofing the book from start to finish. Yes, I think writing a book is a lot like shooting a movie – out of sequence. In the process of proofing, I found myself grabbing a statement in the introduction. The statement is this, "The All-American fairy tale begins and ends with a commitment to stay forever." I began to ponder the difference between the word commitment and interest. There are several things we find ourselves interested in, but it seems that interests only happen when we feel the circumstances are convenient. I am beginning to wonder if the divorce rate has skyrocketed because many mates are "interested" in marriage versus being "committed" to marriage. Commitment, on the other hand, is something you accept with absolutely no excuses, only results. Have you truly committed to love or are you still interested in love? Because until you make the full fledged, no excuses commitment to love one another, your marriage will remain in a holding pattern. Sometimes in our marriages we sit and wait for the feelings to come before we act. That is backwards! We must act towards our commitment to one another and trust that the feelings will come. Our prayer is that you will be willing to get vulnerable with one another about the level of your marriage in order to hold one another accountable, as well as, to impart wisdom from your own marital trials and triumphs into other marriages.

Choose Life

"If I speak in the tongues of men and of angels, but have not love, I am only a resounding gong or a clanging cymbal. If I have the gift of prophecy and can fathom all mysteries and all knowledge, and if I have a faith that can move mountains, but have not love, I am nothing. If I give all I possess to the poor and surrender my body to the flames, but have not love, I gain nothing."
~ 1 Corinthians 13:1-8a and 13

THOUGHT LIFE

THE QUESTION I MUST ASK:

**IS MY MIND BEING FILLED WITH THE
WORLD'S WAY OR GOD'S WAY?**

BATTLE OF THE MIND

"The mind is its own place, and in itself, can make heaven of Hell, and a hell of Heaven." ~ John Milton

The human brain weighs less than three pounds, is made up of 80 percent water and has the texture of jell-o. It would never make it standing alone, yet it is extremely powerful when connected to the neurology of the human body. Several internet sources have researched that the brain allows us to audibly speak at the rate of one hundred and twenty words a minute. However, in our mind we say thirteen hundred words a minute. Out of those thirteen hundred words we say to ourselves, seventy percent of them are negative. My thought, Satan is out to kill, steal and destroy us and he is using the mind to do it. We allow our mind to go rampant. If we are not careful, we believe a lie to be truth so long, that we live that lie out. When Steve was a little boy his Dad would say to him, "Steve, you're a good boy. Good for nothing, but you're a good boy." Everyone would laugh when it was said and for a little while, all you heard was "you're a good boy", but eventually the sounds changed and all you began to hear is "good for nothing." For many years, Steve believed that lie and he lived it out. It is still a struggle to this day in dealing with the confidence to venture into areas of life that aren't familiar.

What lies have you believed to be true that you find yourself living out?

_____

_____

_____

How are those lies holding you back from being all you can truly be?

_____

_____

_____

Our mind never gets to take a vacation. And while that is tough at times, it is also phenomenal that God gave our brains the ability to reason, to make choices, and the ability to love Him and others. There is absolutely no part of our body more important than our brain and to think what all weighs on that three pound mass is more than I can wrap my own mind around. However, there is also no greater target for Satan's arrows. If he can get into your head and destruct the good things, he will own you. He absolutely does not want our minds to work anywhere in the same range as God wants them to work. As we are writing this book, we have grown to understand Satan's ways greater than ever before, especially when dealing with the chapters on thought life. There have literally been times when we would sit here for hours hoping and praying that words would hit the pages and nothing. Where did Satan attack? Yes, you guessed it, the mind. I remember hearing Joann Weaver say once that, "In order to write a book, you have to live the book." Can I just tell you, that is not necessarily a fun feeling and yet it is so true! But imagine what would happen if we took control of the mind away from Satan. Imagine if we made the conscientious choice to plant seeds of good in our minds.

What are you currently planting in your mind?

_____

_____

_____

What feelings overtake your brain that you do not seem to have the power to control? Why not replace those things with God things?

_____

_____

_____

Joyce Meyer writes in <u>Battlefield of the Mind</u>, "I didn't think about what I was thinking about. I simply thought whatever fell into my head. I had no revelation that Satan could inject thoughts into my mind. Much of what was in my head was either lies that Satan was telling me or just plain nonsense, things that were not worth spending my time thinking about. The devil was controlling my life because he was controlling my thoughts." Irresponsible thinking is a dangerous game. As Joanna Weaver says, "For as our thoughts go, so go our emotions. And as our emotions go, so often goes our faith. If the enemy can get me confused, he can get me discouraged. If he can get me discouraged, he can cause me to doubt. If he can make me doubt, he can distract my mind—and that's just a step away from dividing my heart." For many of us we think that as long as our thoughts remain in our heads, they are not harmful to anyone. If that is your way of thinking, you are oh so wrong. If you are thinking about leaving your mate, you will do some stupid things throughout the thought process. Are you thinking about all that the CEO of your company is doing wrong? If so, I can assure you that you are not your best everyday from 9-5. Are you thinking about mistakes you made in the past that you can not move on from? If so, I guarantee much of your down time is spent beating yourself up. Are you thinking about how awesome your life is? If so, I can without a shadow of doubt, guarantee good things are surrounding you.

What is your minds greatest weakness?

_____

_____

_____

What is your minds greatest strength?

_____

_____

_____

Which are you living out most profoundly?

_____

_____

_____

Folks, I realize that not every thought that goes through your head is going to be positive. That is unrealistic, but I also have recognized in my own life that is completely my choice as to what I will allow to stay and run rampant and what I will push away. 2 Corinthians 10:5 states, "We demolish arguments and every pretension that sets itself up against the knowledge of God, and we take captive every thought to make it obedient to Christ." Will you make the choice today to demolish negative thoughts?

Reflection for Direction

The longer Steve and I live the more we realize that life will never be free from tough times. There is always going to be adversity, however, the way our mind processes that adversity will ultimately indicate our rate of growth. The big question, however, is "how do you stay positive when things get rough?" Staying upbeat when the world seems to be crashing in around you seems to be the last thing on your mind, but it should be the first, you need to think positively in the hard times more than at any other time. Life really becomes what you make it and by replacing damaging thoughts with positive ones you have the ability to at least build some strong character. And in the end, God is not real concerned with our comfort but rather that character that can only be built through the tough times. Below are some excellent tips for keeping a positive outlook on life no matter what your circumstances are around you.

• If you find yourself surrounded by negativity break free from it, negativity has a contagious way of passing from one person to another and it will usually bring you further down.
• Take time out of each day to do something that you enjoy doing that doesn't require you to make choices or decisions, but rather relaxes and calms you.
• Try doing something that you wouldn't normally do, something that is totally unlike you and out of character, take up a new hobby or sport that you would never have dreamed of doing.
• Get some exercise, this could be something as simple as taking a walk in the fresh air and is totally free or go to the gym. The natural endorphins that our body produces are a great high.
• Set some realistic goals and when you accomplish a goal give yourself a small reward for doing so.
• Listen to Christian music as it places good thoughts of Biblical truth in your mind.
• Encourage others as it has a way of coming back to you.
• Look for the best in bad situations, while things might not be what we expect if you look hard enough you may find they are not as bad as they seem to be.
• Remember that most tough situations are temporary, so don't let your mind drag you out of the game.

Life Talk

It is very important that we take the time, especially in the midst of our peers where accountability will always be one of the greatest benefits, to figure out why we wrap our mind around things that have no power. Negative thoughts say we have no ability, will never amount to anything and will never be strong enough to conquer adversity. It is so important to discover why you have these thoughts. Many of these thoughts have come from childhood or poor choices we have made as adults that we are unable to forgive ourselves for. Perhaps your mind is filled with negative thoughts because you were overweight as a child, maybe you had a sibling that was smarter than you, maybe you were cut from the baseball team or maybe you came from an abusive family. You must find the cause and you must reprogram the mind. This is not an easy task, but with prayer, perseverance and accountability, it can be done. Give yourself time to work through this as your negative thoughts did not build in one day and they are not going to go away in one day. You, however, will need to make a commitment everyday to become aware of your thoughts and the triggers that stimulate them. Romans 7:22-23 says, "For in my inner being I delight in God's law; but I see another law at work in the members of my body, waging war against the law of my mind and making me a prisoner of the law of sin at work within my members." You are in a war in that you must constantly be aware of. Let's think of a trial as a learning experience and take a journey to get focused toward moving forward.

Name a time when you were able to picture yourself succeeding, even when the odds were stacked against you. (Share details of why you believed you could "do it.")

_____

_____

_____

Write down 5 things for which you each are thankful for.
(This might be a great activity to begin each day with)

_____

_____

_____

Are there positive things that were said to you in the past that still
come to mind? (Voice a positive thought to cancel each negative)

_____

_____

_____

Pray! Who do you trust to stand in the prayer gap for you? Ask
them to pray.

_____

_____

_____

Name some instances in your life that have created a negative
thought stream in your mind. (Remember it is not what happens to
us but rather what is in us that settle our pain and fear)

_____

_____

_____

Are you willing to take a risk and admit what you need from others?

_____

_____

_____

Stop thinking and speaking fearful negative thoughts--start believing good things are going to happen. You cannot have a positive life and a negative mind. Positive thoughts are full of faith, hope and trust in God. In the end, the choice is yours to make.

Choose Life

"For as he thinks within himself, so he is." ~ Proverbs 23:7

DISCONTENTMENT

What does being discontent have to do with your thought life? I'm so glad you asked. Being content actually begins in the mind. Remember that yesterday we talked about how powerful the mind is. Discontentment is actually a desire for something better than your present situation. In our young married years when we had small children, I did not work outside the home. What I found myself doing in my idle time or rather time that did not require a lot of discipline, was thinking and daydreaming. Is it not ironic that what you think you want, to be a stay at home Mom, could cause you to fall into a dangerous place? Thoughts coupled with soap operas and romance novels can lead women to begin to desire an unrealistic life. For men, your time at the office may draw other women's courtesy and interest in your life to make you believe they can provide something for you that your wife can not. The look and dress of other women in the office, at the gym or wherever you find yourself may also turn your thoughts and imagination to an unrealistic place. You do not live with those women, therefore, what you see on the outside looking in is not going to be what your marriage realistically looks like. It will make you look at your life and become very dissatisfied with the reality of the actual life you are living. Isn't it quite paradoxical that some of the very things that create unhappiness are the very things we think will also make things better in our lives?

What things in your life have you become discontent with?

_____

_____

_____

If you are being honest, what have you thought of in the quietness, would make life better?

_____

_____

_____

Life seems safest when we are able to deal with our discontentment by accumulating things. I grew up where I was denied very little of what I "believed" I wanted. We see it in children at Christmas time. They have a list three miles long the moment they are old enough to communicate it, however, they get their "stuff" and spend so little time playing with what they so desperately wanted. Why? Because they grew tired and discontent with things. They realized that the joy they anticipated their new toys to bring them would not. It is not a whole lot different with adults. The unhappier we become the more we believe "stuff" will make us better. But, my friends, I am here to tell you from personal experience that it is only a temporary high. There is the momentary high, but it has never nor will it ever last long enough to satisfy our craving for something more. Please understand there are many ways we play out our discontentment. In being completely real and vulnerable, mine happened to be the pursuit of more things. But, yours might be alcohol, drugs, co-dependency, unhealthy relationships, fitness or eating. And only when you tire of the fact that your drive for something extra in life will not satisfy are you then able to realize that things just aren't working for you or you begin a new pursuit for something else to make life feel more complete.

Maybe you have put the pressure of another human being on your life to satisfy. Maybe you begin to play the "if only" game.

If...Steve would be more romantic
If...Steve would make more money
If...Steve would come home sooner.
If...Steve would talk to me more
If...Steve would pay more attention to me.
If...Steve would be a better Dad

If...Steve would be more successful
If...Steve would buy me a bigger house
If...Steve would buy me a new car
If...Steve would take me on trips
If...Steve would take me out to eat to nice restaurants
If...Debbie would keep the house cleaner
If...Debbie would have dinner ready when I get home from work
If...Debbie would do the laundry
If...Debbie would have sex more often
If...My children would make better grades
If...My children would act better
If...My friends would meet my needs
If...My job would pay more

And the list becomes an unending version of infinity times infinity. Can you relate?

_____

_____

_____

Wow, the burden we place on others can become so tremendous that it has the capability to suck the life out of people. I can visually see the weight I placed on Steve to make me happy. And boy did he try. He wanted my happiness as much as I wanted my happiness. But, in the end, no one can make you happy. It is truly an inside job!

Who are you requiring to make you happy?

_____

_____

_____

Don't you think its time to set them free?

_____

_____

_____

In our selfishness and immaturity, we take years of toil on those we love before we finally release them. My heart hurts as I write this with the realization of the negative impact I had on Steve and my children trying to find contentment. Maybe for you, you can not relate to putting a chain on others, but its time for you to empty the closets of the things you have collected on your search for meaning. Maybe for you, its time you find gratefulness among your current circumstances. Maybe it's not your job or your spouse or your children or your friend or your circumstances that are the problem-maybe it's your attitude. Maybe you are living a life of discontentment because you can not live in the moment for fear of what tomorrow or ten years will bring. Do you understand that God gave us this very moment? He wants us to relish in the miracle of it.

Reflection for Direction

Everyone struggles with discontentment at one time or another. Discontentment will always be with us. At least in this life it is impossible to rid ourselves of it entirely. Chapter 4 in the book of James makes very clear points when speaking about the connection between discontentment and circumstances. We most often feel discontent because we have put our hope in our own ability to create the right circumstances for our lives rather than in God. God never changes, so maybe the change here needs to be an honest heart check. Are you willing to get real with your mate about the level of contentment you have in your relationship with God, with each other and with your present life circumstances?

Life Talk

Discontentment is sin no matter which way you slice it. So, let us take some time in your group to find the root of your discontentment. Here are some helpful questions for you to ask one another:

- Are you putting your hope in the approval of men or the approval of God?
- Are you impatient with faults or inefficiency of others?
- Do you spend time feeling as though you deserve better treatment than you've received?
- Are you filling your mind with books or movies that are giving you unrealistic views of the life you think you want?
- Is the pressure you are putting on others so intense that they will never measure up and as a result you will spend life constantly disappointed?
- Is your life full of turmoil?
- Are you fighting with those you love most due to the fatigue of trying to live a fairy tale life?
- Does your discontentment lead to jealousy or possessiveness?

Choose Life

"What causes fights and quarrels among you? Don't they come from your desires that battle within you? You want something but don't get it. You kill and covet, but you cannot have what you want."
~ James 4:1-2

ADDICTIONS

"You do anything long enough to escape the habit of living until the escape becomes the habit." ~ David Ryan

We all have things that we rely on as our "vices." For some of us it may be addictions that are accepted by the world such as exercise, shopping, coffee, or relationships, whiles others might have addictions that lead to some type of mental or physical unhealthiness. The dictionary defines addiction as the psychological and bodily dependence on a substance or practice which is beyond voluntary control. I think an addiction is anything we feel tempted to lie about. Bottom line, addictions occur when we have an inability to fill a void in our life. Most times the void is caused by the desire to escape reality due to pain of the past or present, boredom or a lack of discipline in our lives. Addictions aid us in continuing to live in the comfort of the past without dealing with the reality of the present. Life is hard! And if life is not hard right now, it will get hard at some point. We can not expect to live in relationship with Christ, follow His will for our lives and it is a piece of cake. Our addictions cause us to live in a fake reality.

What addictions or vices can you identify in your life?

_____

_____

_____

What has caused these addictions to take root in your life?

_____

_____

_____

Honestly, it makes sense why so many people are battling addictions. We are a society that wants the good life free of stresses with all of our wants, needs and desires met instantly. Anne Schaef says it so well in, <u>When Society Becomes An Addict</u>, "Our society is deteriorating at an alarming rate. As we watch the news and read the news papers, we are increasingly made aware of corruption in high places, financial collapse, and a lack of morality in settings ranging from preschools to meat packing plants. As a society, we are responding not with action but with a widespread malaise...Apathy and depression have become synonymous with adjustment. Rather than looking for ways to change, to save ourselves, we are becoming more conservative, more complacent, and more defensive of the status quo."

Think of what an instant gratification society we are. We can literally sit in our pajamas never leaving the comfort of our home and order food to be delivered, shop for things and have them delivered to our door, get an instant response to communication through email, text messages or instant messaging. The media is not helping the cause either. It has embedded in us a message that says we can have anything we want and live any dream we can imagine. Yet, it doesn't teach us how to work through things when the dream doesn't happen. As much as I hate saying this, the church has not helped in this quest. At many churches today, a person with hurts and despairs walks into a religious building and leaves with a message of "give it to Jesus and all will be well." Come on folks, it is simply not that easy. God knew that we would walk through tough times and that the tough times would grow and develop great qualities. And until the church consistently becomes a hospital for sinners instead of a hotel for saints, we as Christians are going to be a detriment to the healing of a lost world. And for people to allow God to help them get through tough times, we have got to show them how to build an emotional connection with Him.

Please understand, in order for anyone to have an emotional connection with God, there must be healthy, Godly people to emotionally connect with us. I can remember when our adoptive daughter first came into our lives, I kept telling her, "In order for you to remove your addictions from your childhood hurts-control, manipulation, selfishness, crisis, arrogance and pride-you need to believe that God can take it all away." She looked at me like I had fourteen heads. Then she said, "Where was your God when I couldn't lay my head down at night as a seven year old? I can't see your God because of what I have seen in people." I thought whoa! But the reality of that is in order for hurting people to know the compassion of God; they must first know the compassion of God's people. The problem with that is that many of God's people are living so superficially that we use that to blanket our own addictions, unable to even begin to help other people see theirs. Then there is another group who are addicted to other people's needs that they lose perspective of their own pitfalls. Come on, we all know these people. They have every answer for every problem for every person, other than themselves.

Are you taking responsibility for your own downfalls or are you living a life that simply points out others downfalls?

_____

_____

_____

Are you helping this world or are you so selfish, critical and cynical that you are the one setting people around you back?

_____

_____

_____

I know this is a hard topic and that words are not being minced here, but folks this is a serious topic. The Suicide Crisis center of Texas states that over 32,000 people a year are taking their lives by suicide. I would be willing to bet that the greatest majority of these people take their lives because the addictions they tried were not enough to mask the pain their insides felt. Please understand the taboo addictions such as alcoholism, gambling, pornography and drugs are serious, but they are not the only problem. Materialism, love of power and control, eating, gossip, shopping, watching television, internet, work, sex and a thousand other issues are also contributing to the lack of willingness to deal with pain in our lives. None of us can eliminate ourselves from this chapter. Addictions are like a serious disease; they are progressive and will lead to death if not actively recovered from. OK, wait so shopping can kill me? Probably not physically, but emotionally, yes, a part of you dies each time you substitute an addiction for truth. OK, but pornography does not hurt anyone, I do it alone in the privacy of my own home. Wrong!! It is putting your marriage in a place where your wife will never measure up to the images you see. And here's one for you, if it is not that big a deal, then why not pull it up when your wife and daughter are in the room. Ouch!

We all have struggled in our life with something that we looked for to fill our lives and make us happy and content. "Until we come to the place of allowing God to complete us, every relationship we have, will be an attempt to complete us." Steve and I use that statement a lot because we could see in our own life how we played that out. Steve and I both ran from our pain or emptiness and instead of running to the big addictions, we turned to the safe ones. Steve looked to me to fill his voids and he turned to his work to find worth and importance. Steve struggled with insecurity that stemmed from no one in his family ever saying anything to build him up. The philosophy of his family was, don't build anyone up or they may take advantage of you. Who knows why they behaved this way, but I am sure somewhere along the way, they were taken advantage of, so the ones who really got hurt through this, were their children. It has been a life struggle for Steve to overcome this need for worth and attention. His Mom was addicted to going to the doctor. She was so hungry for attention that she made up aliments to get that attention from the doctors and others. When you live in an environment like that for years, you pass on such unhealthy characteristics. Can you see how Steve turned to people to complete him when all along his completeness could only be met by God, who pours more worth and value into us than we can grasp. Once that is grasped, you can live with people accepting you or rejecting you, it really makes life ok. Otherwise, your whole life is consumed with trying to get the attention of others or to beg for affirmations. It is so childlike, yet we have so many adults with childlike behaviors.

When I was growing up, I loved attention as well. Maybe we need to stop right now and recognize that children need desperately to have the attention and affection of their parents. If they do not get that attention, where or what is it going to lead them into? How did I live out my neglect of positive attention? I turned to the church and to guys. Anything I needed, I thought I could find it through others. When you are starved for attention, you will many times make wrong choices. And these choices will always carry long term consequences. I made it through my early years with little consequences; however, my brother has struggled all his life. The place where he found the most attention was at the casinos. Yes, my brother was a gambling addict. I have watched him spiral down, down, down all of his life, just for some attention. He told me once that walking into a casino made him feel so important. If he went to the same one, they always knew his name and made him feel like he was the most important person in the world. People will do anything or go anywhere for that feeling. If the addiction is not dealt with, no matter what age you are, you will continually look for that void to be filled. I am happy to tell you that my brother, at the age of 55, is finally at the bottom and is turning to the only one who can give him everything he needs - God. He is finally seeing that God loves him, even through his bad choices, and that he is worthy and significant to God no matter who he is or what he does. His completeness is finally coming from the only one that can give it to him.

Would you be willing to look into your own life? Are you leaning strongly on others to give you significance?

_____

_____

_____

Some days you will get it and even feel that you have conquered your addiction without the help of anyone, but it will not sustain you because it can not. When God made us, He made our heart with a hole that only He could fill. He also gave us the ability to choose, so you have to choose to allow God to fill your voids. Once you have made the God choice, your fate is sealed for as long as you choose to believe what He says and feels about you. God backs this up when he says in 2 Corinthians 12:9-10, "My grace is sufficient for you, my power is made perfect in weakness; therefore, I will boast all the more gladly about my weaknesses, so that Christ's power may rest on me. That is why, for Christ's sake, I delight in weakness, in insults, in hardships, in persecutions, in difficulties. For when I am weak, then I am strong."

Reflection for Direction

One addiction we can all relate to is the approval of man. All of us want someone to approve of us. This starts when we are a child and hope that someone will think enough of us to be their friend. We take this cycle into our job interviews, our marriages, and friendships. The need for approval begins with our parents and if they did not approve of us, we will seek to find it elsewhere. Maybe in your marriage one of you grew up with all the approval in the world and the other one grew up with no approval. If you are not careful, one mate will become frustrated as they diligently strive to give you all the approval they think you need, and all the while it is never enough. The need for approval and recognition can be a vicious cycle. The more Steve and I feel each other's approval for one another, the more we are able to understand and feel God's approval which allows peace to be the central core of our lives, giving us the ability then to give others the approval they need.

Life Talk

How has the lack of approval or the abundance of approval affected your life? Your marriage? Your relationship with others?

Let's refer back to our characters from the movie, *City Slickers*. The first character felt approval by the time his Dad spent taking him to a baseball game and the physical touch when his Dad held his hand. The second character felt approval by the wink of his Dad and the third character felt approval when he was able to stand up to his Dad. One recognized approval by a touch, one recognized approval by an action and one recognized approval by words. Now look at your life. How do you most feel approval? The problem with many marriages today is that we are giving our mate the type of approval we need because that is most comfortable for us, however, what we need to be giving is the type of approval that meets the needs of our mate.

Choose Life

"I keep asking that the God of our Lord Jesus Christ, the glorious father, may give you the spirit of wisdom and revelation, so that you may know him better." ~ Ephesians 1:17

IN THE BEDROOM

"God designed sex for oneness in marriage. He designed it as a means of intimate communication between a man and a woman who have committed themselves to each other for life. In any other context, the purpose of sex gets twisted."
~ William Cutrer

Is it not an amazing statistic that sex is only 5 percent of your marriage, yet when it is not working; it becomes 95 percent of your marriage? Many marriages today are living in such dysfunction and unfortunately much of this is due to barriers that affect us in the bedroom. God created sex and He created it to be something good and healthy within the framework of marriage. He made it for His children to enjoy and to intimately experience the body becoming one flesh. It is an amazing phenomenon!

How were you brought up to view sex? How has your viewpoint positively or negatively affected your sex life?

_____

_____

_____

While we are dating we can not seem to keep our hands off of one another. We become married and while this transgression seems as though it is never going to decline, it almost always does in marriage. We get busy, we have children, we lose the emotional connection that pulled us so close together in the beginning and before we know it, we have given up our physical relationship and it seems like several other emotions leave with it. The unfortunate thing is that some marriages lose this early on due to the pain in their lives they have never dealt with. Are you beginning to see the repetitiveness of "pain of the past?" As much as we hate to say it that is probably the consistent issue that has the ability to affect every mosquito in this book. Steve and I met with a young couple recently that is newly married. There is nothing happening sexually in their marriage because so many walls have built up from a lack of communication and forgiveness. When our relationship is not what it is supposed to be, the first thing that goes is sex!

Has your sex life been affected due to the lack of one partner or both having unresolved pain of the past? Would you be willing to identify the pain?

_____

_____

_____

It is a natural progression as a couple falls in love with one another to move into a physical direction. It is like you can't get enough of one another. If many marriages begin with a strong desire to be sexual then what happens over time? We need to look at a couple of factors that cause this area of marriage to go south. One is our perception of sex. This is an area primarily directed toward women. I was raised in a very strict Baptist home and church. I was taught that sex was an ugly thing, even nasty and that good girls abstained from such actions. Ok, that was fine as a young single girl, but how was I then suppose to take that information and transfer it in my mind as something good as I am about to marry? How are we supposed to spend years thinking one way and then after we say "I Do" everything changes? The transition worked the first couple of months of marriage and then the old mind started working. I thought things like, "Am I only important to Steve for my body as it seems that is all he is interested in?" If I touch him in any way it leads to sex, therefore, the church must have been right. This is not a good thing! Girls begin to make excuses when their husbands make advances. "Oh honey, I have a headache, or I'm just too tired!" My excuse to Steve was that all day I had children crawling all over me, and the last thing I needed was him doing the same. BOOM! Here is where the hurts, rejection and neglect begin. The real issue was in my mind but what I created was a deep root of rejection in Steve's life. The Bible says specifically, not to forsake this area in our marriage. God knew it would cause all kinds of problems and wow has it ever. Today, because there is a stand off in the bedroom, more and more affairs are happening. There is even an unhealthy emotional connection with our children. It has caused men and women to look at pornography and attach themselves to fake people with no emotional connection. We are living in a world of incest and childhood sexual molestation and on and on we can go. When we walk outside of God's principles, we enter into a world of evil and sin. Therefore, we must go back to God's word and remember that God created this area of marriage as something good. When the sexual relationship is working well, then all other aspects of marriage seem to work better. We must allow God to change any hang ups that we have in our mind.

What lies have you believed about sex? Don't you think it's time to hand those over to God and allow him the opportunity to change your thinking?

_____

_____

_____

I began to take this seriously and begin to pray and ask God to give me the desire for Steve sexually. He spoke to me one day reminding me that of all the women in the world, Steve chose me to meet his physical needs. When I really gave that a lot of THOUGHT, it changed my heart towards him. I made the choice to change my perceptions of sex and realize that God wanted us to enjoy one another without shame. Steve needed a responsive wife, not a dead wife.

Another perception that has to change is the fact that God can forgive any of our past mistakes or change our heart if we have been a victim of a wrongful sexual encounter. Because man has walked away from God, there are consequences to our choices. Many people that love God, made the mistake of engaging in pre-marital sex. At the time, we could not see the damage it could do one day to our marriage, but slowly it creeps in leaving us with regrets, shame and guilt. Please hear us, God is not in guilt. God set His people free and that is what He desires for his children. Much of the time, it is not about God forgiving us, we have to come to the place where we forgive ourselves. Ezekiel 36:26 says, "I will give you a new heart and put a new spirit in you; I will remove from you your heart of stone and give you a heart of flesh."

That's great guys, but now what? Where do we go from here? There is no possible way for us to identify every issue that couples have in the area of sex; however, I think we can all agree that much of the confusion and frustration has begun in our mind. For women, sex starts in our heads, unlike men, who see it as a physical act. It is not uncommon for a woman to detach from her husband physically because her perception may be that all he is interested in is a physical relationship. A woman, most likely, will not engage in healthy sex without an emotional connection. Let's take a journey back to the dating years. Men, you gave lots of attention, affection, care and consideration during the courtship. I can almost guarantee you these characteristics aroused the sexual feelings in your wife. We marry and become busy with the day to day aspects of life and in the midst of this, many of you stopped doing the things that attracted us so much to you and thus, there is no sexual response from your wife that there once was. Women want a passionate feeling in their marriage, but without the essential ingredients to get there, it just doesn't happen.

Sex is a hard emotion to keep consistent under normal life circumstances, but a battle of bitterness or resentment going on will almost always impact the desire to have sex. If you are going to live with someone, it is impossible to move through life without hurting one another. The key to this is building healthy conflict by taking the time to apologize to one another while also discussing things that are hard for you each to deal with so that underlying hurt does not deter from a healthy sexual relationship.

Are you someone who finds it easy to say, "I'm sorry?" If it is difficult for you to say "I'm sorry," why is it difficult?

_____

_____

_____

The more people we counsel, the more I am amazed at the number of people who harbor anger or are more comfortable in crisis then peace. God said in Ephesians 4:26, "Never let the sun go down on your anger." God knew that our anger would separate a marriage emotionally and eventually lead to destruction. We must put our pride down if we are ever going to accept honesty and extend forgiveness.

If you were willing to be completely honest and real, how is your marriage? Are their underlying currents that you have chosen to sweep under the rug because it is easier than dealing with them?

_____

_____

_____

Is there an openness to discuss the physical relationship in marriage or is your marriage full of guilt and frustration and nothing is ever verbalized?

_____

_____

_____

Please hear us again, your sexual relationship is only 5% of a marriage, but if it is not working properly it is 95% of a marriage. Start a discussion today about this part of your marriage. There could certainly be something wrong physically, but the majority of the time a woman is disconnected due to lack of emotions and a man is disconnected due to rejection or negative words.

Reflection for Direction

Steve and I spend 10-15 hours a week in counseling sessions. It breaks our hearts to witness couple after couple come to us due to frustration with life in the bedroom. We take a major expectation into our marriage believing we will have years of passionate sex. The disappointment felt when this expectation is unmet is equal between men and women. I am certain that God intended for this to be one of the sweetest aspects of our marriage as he left us with inspiration in the book, *Song of Solomon*, where a sweet physical relationship is depicted between a man and his wife. Maybe it's time for each of us to go back and read that book with a clear understanding of how a man is to love his wife and long for her and in doing that it arouses her appetite for him. Today, we have given our minds free reign to move away from the purity of that book. Television, movies and books have entered our minds and have caused us to look at sex as a means to satisfy our own needs and not the needs of our mate. Love has turned into lust, giving into getting and lasting commitment into "no strings attached." Will you allow God to bring your marriage back to the place where we desire to love each other physically because of a deep love we share for one another spiritually and emotionally?

Life Talk

Sex in marriage is a very private and personal issue and is probably not at the top of the list of what we are comfortable sharing. Can we beg of you to open up with restraint and respect so that you may gain freedom in this area? We suggest that you share only what is agreed upon as a husband and wife and that each of you remain respectful of everyone in your community group. The questions below are a means to get you engaged in a healthy discussion. Have there been some years where sex in our marriage was non-existent? What obstacles were causing this? What do you need from your mate to move you towards a healthy physical relationship?

Choose Life

"I am my lover's and my lover is mine, he browses among the lilies."
~ Song of Solomon 6:3

SURRENDER OF THE MIND

"Change is the essence of life. Be willing to surrender what you are for what you could become." ~ Author Unknown

The mind, no doubt, can be the greatest asset God has given us, however it can also be an enemy full of destructive ways. We must acknowledge the fact that the mind is a dangerous thing when left to freely think. My friends, careless thinking is a dangerous habit that has brought down many men. Have you ever been in a conversation with someone and when the conversation begins, you are certain they are wrong; however, as your mind begins to get tainted, you slowly begin to doubt yourself? I can remember vividly this happening to me. Steve and I went one weekend to a Bed and Breakfast in Natchitoches, LA. The owner of the B & B loved to sit and visit. We visited about our children, our communities, our interests and our marriage ministry. After a bit, she asked us if we had read <u>The Davinci Code</u>. We had not. She responded by saying, "Oh, you must go get it and read it. It will really make you wonder about some things." What did I do? I went home and bought the book.

Are you easily swayed by the opinions and mindset of others?

_____

_____

_____

The book quickly caught my attention, so much so, that I could not put it down. After I had read seventy five percent of the book, I found myself questioning a truth that has been my foundation for my entire life. Steve, on the other hand, was not influenced at all by the author's take on Jesus. I had given my mind to someone else's theology and as a result, it began to divide my heart. If we are not constantly aware, we will find ourselves giving our minds to other people's opinions, thoughts, desires and demands. It says in 2 Corinthians 10:5, "To demolish arguments and every pretension that sets itself up against the knowledge of God and take captive every thought." We must demolish thoughts that do not line up with God's teachings and principles. Demolish means to tear down, smash and destroy.

What thoughts do you need to demolish in order to realign your mind with God's ways and truths?

_____

_____

_____

In order for us to completely demolish rampant and unhealthy thoughts, we must spend time in God's word and be able to seek His truth when we are weak. The bible is full of knowledge and truth we are to live out, but how are we to live out, that which we have not spent any time learning? If you have grown up around church, you have probably heard the saying, "people can tell where your heart is by looking in your checkbook." What would people say about your heart by looking into your mind? Whether you believe it or not, what goes on in your mind will become a large part of your heart. Many of you are thinking that sounds simple enough, while others of you may not even have a clue where to start. Read the Bible every day so that a seed of God's words is planted in you each day. If you are unfamiliar with the Bible or unsure what to read, begin by simply reading a Proverbs each day. If the date is the 10th of the month, read Proverbs Chapter 10 and so forth as it will give you simple and real life principles to live by. Choose a book of the Bible that you are going to read through. I had an amazing mentor who taught me to read one verse and stay there until it takes root in my life and I am able to live it out. This has taught me how to understand and grasp how alive God's word is and how it still holds true in our lives today. Please hear us, your quiet time each day should not be a time where you sit, read, close the Bible and then go on checking it off your "To Do" list. Rather, it is meant to slowly absorb and then be an asset that determines how we will treat others, solve problems, trust, spend our money, grieve and deal with conflict, worry and anxiety.

In order to fully discuss surrender, we must talk about pride. Pride will absolutely be the greatest deterrent in surrendering. Many of you have grown up believing that surrendering is failure and failure leads to weakness. However, there will be no growth that takes place in our lives without admitting our failure and the sin in our lives. We are a broken people, in love with ourselves, full of selfishness, desires and negative thoughts and until we surrender those to true brokenness, our hearts will always be corroded. Check out what James says in Chapter 3:13-18. He hammers us when he says, "Who is wise and understanding among us? Let him show it by his good life, by deeds done in the humility that comes from wisdom. But if you harbor bitter envy and selfish ambition in your hearts, do not boast about it or deny the truth. Such wisdom does not come from heaven but is earthly, unspiritual, of the devil. For where you have envy and selfish ambition, there you find disorder and every evil practice." We do not have to look far to see this lived out. Many of America's leaders today are prideful and arrogant, speaking lies that promote themselves. Look at churches, schools, sports teams and corporate CEO's all around you, just to name a few. While many of these agencies leaders are tremendous, there are also those with narcissistic tendencies void of humility.

Who do you know that is a humble leader? What makes them humble? What qualities are you willing to learn from their willingness to surrender to humility?

_____

_____

_____

Can Steve and I be so bold, as to throw a statement out that we are almost certain is true? If you struggle to surrender because of pride and selfishness, God will continue to put people over you with the same qualities that you struggle with because sometimes that is the only mirror we are willing to look into. We have seen this in our own lives as well as the lives of our grown children. When any of our minds have been loaded with pride, selfishness or disorder, God has put leaders over us with the same exact qualities and means to play those qualities out. Are you in a job you hate because your boss is narcissistic, brash or demeaning? Look first to see if you are there because you will not surrender on your own. Are your children out of control? Look to see if their behavior is a reflection of the things stirring in your own mind and heart. Have you been married 3 times and still can not understand why you are at the crossroads of another divorce? Look to see what role you are playing in that separation or even better, look at the things in your mind that are causing you to make bad choices in a mate. Proverbs 29:23 states, "A man's pride brings him low, but a man of lowly spirit gains honor." Is the mind a powerful key to our lives? You better believe it absolutely is and if you deny it, you are sunk!

Reflection for Direction

Psalms 119:11 says. "I have hidden your word in my heart that I might not sin against you." Our **ONLY** option for peace is to memorize not only what scripture says, but what it means. Would you be willing to read your Bible everyday for 30 days and journal the difference it makes in your heart? I believe that what you will find is that not only will you be at peace, but you will also infect others with that same peace creating a catalyst for change around you. Discipline your mind to memorize scriptures that hit you in your current situation. Place those scriptures on note cards and take them with you so that you are able to memorize them allowing them to penetrate your being. You may memorize certain scriptures for a period of time and then not read them again for some time, however, you will have an encounter where you need to draw wisdom and immediately they will come back to mind. God is actively asking us to know him intimately and to know him; we must spend time with him to know what He feels and thinks. He says in Isaiah 41:9-10, "I took you from the ends of the earth, from its farthest corners I called you. I said, 'You are my servant'; I have chosen you and have not rejected you. So do not fear, for I am with you; do not be dismayed, for I am your God." God chose you and because of that, He will never leave you. Rest in that!

Life Talk

If we are being completely honest with one another, our weakest link as Christians is the lack of knowing God and his ways and words. We see this when it comes to our own problems, as well as, times we are dealing with the discomfort of other's hurts. We are void of ways to guide or direct them because we have not taken the time to draw from God's wisdom. We are not asking you to surrender something based on what we believe or what your peers in your group believe, but rather on something *you* have grasped and trust your mind to. Maybe is time for you to begin reading the book of John. If you will begin to let Jesus' words through John penetrate your heart, you will grasp the fact that God is pursuing you and desiring to love you to the place of surrender. When you need wisdom and discernment, where do you turn? Can you find the answers you need in the Bible or do you feel lost to find them? Do you trust the word of God to give you the answers you need? Examine your fears and expound on them.

Choose Life

"He humbled you, causing you to hunger and then feeding you with manna, which neither you nor your fathers had known, to teach you that man does not live on bread alone but on every word that comes from the mouth of the Lord." ~ Deuteronomy 8:3

FORGIVENESS

THE QUESTION I MUST ASK:

DO WE LOVE EACH OTHER ENOUGH TO FORGIVE THOSE WHO HAVE DEEPLY WOUNDED OUR PAST?

PAIN OF THE PAST

"If we are not careful we clutch the past so tightly that we are unable to open our arms and embrace the future."

Forgiveness means letting go of the past. The problem is that many of us have never even taken a journey back to the past to identify what it is that we are being held in bondage by. The first word of this title is why we do not want to go back. It hurts! It hurt then, and we stay in denial of the past because we know that it might hurt even worse to go back. You must go back, or you will not be able to love, walk with God or move forward. Some of you may not believe that you have been wounded by pain of the past. It is impossible to live in a sinful world and not experience some kind of hurt in your life. Some of your families may have given you tools to deal with the wounds, however, others of you may have never been given tools and therefore, you sit so wounded that you wonder if life will ever contain joy.

Take the time to identify some hurts that immediately come to mind.

_____

_____

_____

Have you healed from these hurts or are you being held prisoner to them?

_____

_____

_____

For me, I immediately think of something that seems so small and insignificant and yet it took hold of my thoughts for so many years. When I was in high school I was a little chunky. I was in the choir and we had a Christmas party. We had drawn names and each of us were to bring a gift to the person whose name we had drawn, but we were not to put our own name on the gift we were giving. It came my turn and I excitedly opened my gift only to find that the person who gave it to me had given me a box of diet chocolates. Can I just tell you that until I was willing to let that go, I'm pretty sure that I punished other people around me for the pain I felt that day? The moral of the story, sometimes the pain we feel may not be identified with someone whose parents have abandoned or abused them, yet it is still pain that we must work through.

Have you kept some pain unidentified because you felt it was insignificant compared to the pain of others?

_____

_____

_____

Steve and I want to get personal with you and tell you about a very tough journey God called us to thirteen years ago from the writing of this book that forever changed the way we both would come to understand pain from the past and the agonizing hurt it does to both the person hurt and the people who are surrounded by the victim and yet, the unbelievable power of God in the moment of forgiveness and healing. Steve and I were serving at a church in Albuquerque, NM and in 1995 we were called to a church in Shreveport, LA. There were times we were not sure why Shreveport, but when God calls you, you go. Our boys were very good soccer players and so one of the first things we did when we arrived in Shreveport was find the best place for them to play and be successful. To our amazement and sometimes doubt, there was a young woman in her mid-twenties who was the Director of Coaching for the select soccer club. In order to play soccer at the highest level in Shreveport, our boys would need to play for this club. We had asked around and found out that the 5'2", fiery female,

Shelley McMillian, was one of the best in the state and would be coaching our oldest son, Josh and was the Director over the coach of our youngest son's, Jordan's, team. We honestly could not have been prepared for the journey that would take place next because of our boy's involvement in the club. Our boys played their first year and while we did not get to know Shelley very well, she did seem to hang around our family on many occasions. I am going to let Shelley join me in telling the story that has still today, changed many lives.

Shelley: I grew up in a home that was certainly not ideal. My biological mother lost her mom when she was four years old, so I'm not sure that she ever truly knew how to nurture me. My biological father was a successful businessman but suffered from alcoholism and drug abuse. My parents divorced when I was six years old and I sometimes feel that experience grew me up faster than kids are born to grow up. Of course, it could have also been the abuse I suffered. My biological mother was emotionally abusive or maybe the way I like for it to sound as I have tried many years to justify an ends to a mean is that she was emotionally unavailable. My biological father was a different story. I strived my whole life to be what would make him proud and because athletics was his thing, even as a young child, I trained diligently to become the athlete that he once was. As I write this, I am saddened by the reality that I was a byproduct of two adults who were either never guided to deal with their own painful pasts or that simply decided it was not worth the pain. So, as in all situations such as this, the cycle continued. My father began sexually abusing me when I was five years old and continued until I was thirteen.

Its ironic and quite paradoxical, he abused me and yet, it never made me falter from trying to be what I thought would make him love me more. Therefore, I continued the cycle of success that I watched him live in his own life. I began playing soccer and I played it with every ounce of survival in me and then when that was not enough, I began my coaching career at seventeen years old. In essence, it became my survival through success. And because it was my survival, I was unhealthily good at it. As I graduated from high school, I began to pull away from the closeness I once was addicted to with my father (At this time, I had resolved to the fact that my mother just couldn't give me anything emotional so I checked out) and yet, the distance did not take away the craving to be close to him. I can remember my first college game as though it were yesterday, not so much for the soccer but because the words that my father spoke to me that day will forever be emblazoned on my heart. I'm sure that this day was the beginning of the downward spiral that I would watch life take me to. We were playing the University of West Florida. I was the only senior and the only local player on my college team, a team that was statistically picked to go 0-16 because this was the inaugural year of the program. To make a long story short, I scored the game winner and was stoked. If you have ever played athletics, it was one of those moments where you are at an all time high and nothing can take the buzz off of your adrenaline rush. I walked off the field and out of the corner of my eye I saw that my father had come to the game. I think I can count on one hand the total number of games that my biological parents came to watch, so seeing him was a bit surreal. He walked over to me and the only words he offered were this, "You weren't in as good a shape as the other players and just so you know, you will never make a living knocking that little round ball around." Folks, as though life had not been hard enough, on that day, in that soccer stadium, I checked out and the emptiness of life was only covered by the success that would take place the next few years of my life. I coached and I won and I won and I won. I drove myself, I drove players, I drove other coaches and the empty well inside of me grew deeper and deeper and deeper. In 1996, I finally reached the ultimate coaching goal of winning a state championship and while I thought winning would fill the holes they only grew emptier and emptier.

In October of that particular year, I resolved to the fact that I would never outlive the pain. I would never outlive the injustices done to me and I would never understand how to be a wife, a mom, a friend, a daughter, a sister or a coach. What simply looked to be success in my life was merely a curtain covering what I did not desire for others to see. So, on October 16th, I woke up, I wrote my own obituary, I bought a gun and prepared for what would finally be the end of a life of pain.

Debbie: I was at a time in my life where I was simply going through the motions. Being the wife of a minister, I think I simply had become numb to some of what God was asking of me. I was coasting along not making a real difference around me. Things appeared to be good on the outside as I sought out a life of significance. Steve and my marriage had been mended and we were at a good place in spending the necessary time together to be connected, but there seemed to be shallowness to our faith. Little did we know that God was about to deepen our relationship with him while also giving us a greater understanding of his wisdom, grace and mercy. On this particular October day, I had gone to lunch with a friend of mine and was headed to Service Merchandise to buy a vacuum cleaner. On my way to the store, I must admit that I had not heard God speak to me as profoundly as he spoke to me in the moment when he told me to turn the car around and go to the school where Shelley McMillian worked. I immediately began to argue with God justifying my reason for not going; reasons such as, I really need to get the vacuum cleaner right now, I have never been to that school before and I don't even know her that well. I called Steve and told him and in his infinite and Godly wisdom he said, "What are you waiting for?" You see, Steve has been in this position many times where God has placed someone on his heart and it has become second nature for him to call them or visit them. For me, this was completely new territory. I was full of questions, doubt and fear and Steve guided me to a place to realize that I simply needed to go and God would handle the rest. As a control freak, it was definitely not something I was comfortable with doing. I, however, went. I got to the school and found Shelley sitting in the gym at the top of the bleachers with kids playing a game down on the floor. I walked to the top of the bleachers (mind you, with her looking at me like she could care less if I lived or died) and did not get a warm and fuzzy feeling. I will never forget the look on her face as I said, "I don't know why I'm here. I was on my way to Service Merchandise and God told me to come here and find you." I wanted to turn around and get out of there as fast as I could, but that would have been even more awkward. I stayed for two hours and never got beyond small talk with a person who had a chip on her shoulder as wide as the Great Wall of China. I left there after two hours feeling as though I had done nothing. I called Steve again and in his infinite wisdom, he simply said, "Ok Jesus, Jr. get out of the way and let God do his thing."

Shelley: Ok honestly, I am sitting at the top of the bleachers minding my own business and this (ok not right, I know) woman I hardly know and am not sure at this point, I want to know comes into the gym I am teaching in and starts talking this God psycho babble about supposedly needing to come and find me. People, I am five hours away from driving to a local lake and blowing my brains out and to be frank, I did not care what Jesus told her. Besides, where was her Jesus when I was a ten years old and could not lay my head down at night for fear of what the night would behold? However, I sat through the next couple of hours with an acquaintance I barely knew, headed out to the soccer field for a training session and then left to go to a local lake in preparation of ending the pain. I must admit I was ticked that someone tried to rain on my parade. One mile from the lake, my cell phone rang and it is her (you know, the lady who won't mind her own business) and she says, "Hey Shell, I just wanted to call and let you know we love you and we are here for you if you need us." I threw her no bones. I drove to the lake and reality began to sit in due to her visit and phone call. It was the kind of reality that makes you think, "I don't even know how you shoot yourself. What if I shoot myself and I don't kill myself, then what?" I pondered that thought for several hours until eventually my fear of failing overtook me and I left the lake. I began the process of muddling through the next few days fighting suicide because I knew it had to be less painful than what I was presently feeling.

Have you wondered where God is in your pain?

_____

_____

_____

Do you know God exists, but wonder if He even cares?

_____

_____

_____

Has God blessed you with a life free of much pain and called you to walk with someone else in their pain?

_____

_____

_____

Reflection for Direction

Life is the only art that we are required to practice without walking through it beforehand. We are not given preliminary trials, failures or botches that are essential in training for a sport, a musical talent or a speaking engagement. We must take life as it comes and fight through to make the choice to allow God to buffer our pain.

List 5 things that have caused you grief, pain, hurt, rejection or failure:

1.

2.

3.

4.

5.

God never wastes a hurt. In the things you listed, can you see how God has used that in your life? If you are not able to see that your pain has made an impact anywhere, it is time for you to pray for God to use your pain to create a ministry rather than misery.

Life Talk

Consider Joseph for a moment. Joseph was the son of Jacob and Rachel. The story is told in Genesis 37. He was a loved and favored child by his father, which caused a lot of anger, bitterness and resentment by his eleven brothers.

Have you ever been on one of those sides? Were you the favored one or the one resented? How did you deal with it? Do not limit yourself to your parents as some of your resentment or favoritism could have come on the heels of a job, another relationship or a friendship. Have you ever wondered why life just seems to never be fair for you?

Can you imagine how Joseph must have felt when there was so much anger directed toward him? I wonder what the emotions were when Joseph was sold to the Ishmaelites to be taken into Egypt to be sold into slavery. On the other hand, what were the emotions of the brothers' who must have realized they had done something terribly wrong? They immediately had to start lying; surely they were overcome with great guilt.

How did Joseph have the ability, at seventeen years, old to make good choices in dealing with his pain? All we know from the Bible is that God was with him and prospered him everywhere he went. I am assuming here, but that had to be Joseph's choice to push through these tough times. What do you think? Do you realize that just as God was with Joseph, he is also with you?

Choose Life

"For just as we share abundantly in the sufferings of Christ, so also our comfort abounds through Christ." ~ 2 Corinthians 1:5

BRIDGE TO LIVE

"He who cannot forgive others, destroys the bridge over which he himself must pass." ~ George Herbert

Go with us to the Royal Gorge. Standing above the Colorado's Wild Arkansas River is a bridge built in 1929. It is the world's highest suspension bridge at 1,260 feet long, 18 feet wide and towering 150 feet high. The bridge is made of 1,300 tons of steel and the walkway has 1,292 planks of deck. The original cost of building the bridge was $350,000 in 1929 and today would cost over $15,000,000. The bridge will support in excess of two million pounds and those who have ventured across it, whether walking or driving, say the experience is priceless. While we are in awe of such a historical site, the bridge is not fail proof. However, the bridge that God built can not and will not fail. It is strong enough to hold our hurts, our pain and our fears.

The Royal Gorge is 1,053 feet down to the bottom and 1,053 feet back to the top. Let's pretend God has built a rope bridge across the Gorge and he asks us to leave all of our hurts and pain and fears on one side of that bridge and trust him enough to walk across that bridge. It is a long scary walk across the bridge because you are holding onto wobbly hand ropes and footholds yet the entire time, God is whispering, "Trust me and walk with me to the other side." Once we get to the other side God hands us an axe and tells us to cut the hand holds and then he takes the axe and cuts the foot holds. He invites us into a world that He has had planned for us to live in all along. Some of us, however, only know how to live with the pain, hurt, fears and crisis and because of this we are going to want to go back and pick that which has been most familiar to ours life back up. Hear us, though, it is a ¼ mile down to the bottom of the Royal Gorge and ¼ mile back up with the weight of the past weighing down the trek. Is it really worth the trip? If we are not careful we get so comfortable with our baggage that we live the abnormal so long we think it is normal. Folks, it takes a tremendous amount of time and energy to release the baggage of your past and yet, many of us will spend more time going back and picking it back up because we have convinced ourselves the abnormal is all we are equipped to handle.

What are you clinging to right now that you need to let go of in order to move forward in your life?

_____

_____

_____

What keeps you from trusting, that once the baggage is on the other side of the Gorge, God can get you through without you having to go back?

_____

_____

_____

Just as a gem cannot be polished without friction, we as humans were made to be perfected through trials. But so many times we give up the refining process because we are in denial. Denial is all you knew as a child to help you avoid the pain, denial is all you knew when your spouse cheated, denial is all you knew when you had the miscarriage, denial is all you knew when your friend hurt you, denial is all you knew when you got fired from your job, but the hard fact and the reality is that you will not make any progress toward healing as long as you continue on your path of denial. Denial has helped many of us survive the hardest parts of life, but if we do not come face to face with the giants of our past, we will never be free from the bondage. Join us as we share our own denial in the process of our journey toward learning about not only forgiveness but the chance to get across a bridge of pain, depression and anger to the other side where great love and life abound.

Shelley: As I muddled through the next few days after that October 16th, I did not know how I would survive, but with everything in me, I knew that the rubber had met the road and somewhere I could find a small piece of hope through the visit of Debbie Wilson or it was simply time to succeed in my original plan. I received a phone call from the Wilson's a few days after October 16th, asking me if I would come to their house and visit with them. I was not sure I had a real peace about that decision but then I also did not have peace about anything, therefore, I went. We sat in their living room and began to talk. I laugh today at God's breaking of my heart and soul, because I was so hard and cold that I can not even imagine what it must have been like to sit in a room with me. They began asking me questions about my past and in a very brash way I said, "My parents abused me. Such is life. It happens to people all the time; I just need to get over it." After what seemed like an hour or two of getting no where, Steve said, "Shell, I don't have the answers and Deb doesn't have the answers, but I know who does." My thought was **finally**, someone with some answers. Steve said, "Shell Jesus loves you and he was there the whole time." At that point, I was done! I got up, said, thank you for your time, but I am not interested in a God that abandoned me when I was unable to protect myself as a child. I rose to leave and Deb said, "Can I hug you?" To which I responded very coldly, "You can do whatever you want!" She pulled me into her lap and I broke twenty years of tears. I must have laid there for two hours with the flood gates open. After a while, the sweetest man I have come to know, laid his head next to mine on the floor and said, "Shell, I know you don't understand this right now, but trust me when I tell you that Jesus was with you every time you were abused. One day you are going to do something so great in your life and you are going to look back to your childhood and be grateful that you went through it." I'm sure he had good intentions and while I wanted to believe him and cling to his words, I was not even in the same hemisphere to be able to grasp even an ounce of what the man was saying to me. After a little while he laid his sweet head down on the floor next to mine and said, "Shell, Jesus wants to take all your pain away. Would you like to ask Him to come and live inside you?" I said, "I have absolutely nothing to lose at this point." That night, on that living room floor, I truly met Jesus for the first time and while I would love to tell you life was immediately transformed and the hurt was gone, but that would not be fair for me to lie to those of you reading this book. I can, however, tell you that it was the seed that would propel me into the hardest next two years of my life.

Debbie: I called Shell a few days after that October 16th because she had briefly told me that her parents had abused her and I sensed she was not okay and my hope and desire was that Steve could give her answers. I felt an urgency to stay in contact with Shell because something in my spirit told me she could slip away at any moment. Shell came to our house, and it was so funny to me, because I had asked her to come so Steve could help her, but then I gave Steve a lecture about what I wanted him to say and what I did not want him to say. I think the beginning of this week set me into a tailspin of realizing that my own faith was shallow and yet God was calling me to seek answers so I could help her. I was uncertain and doubtful, Shell would show up at our house, but she did and from there I knew that every word we said would be dependent on her staying or leaving. Honestly, I have never been around a harder person in my life and I think the reason is because it was typical of me to pick people to help where I knew I would be successful. As the night went on, I knew once Steve told Shell about Jesus that she was turned off and in a panic attempt, I knew I had to do something so I said, "Can I hug you?" It seemed like Shell cried for a long time and wow, was I uncomfortable with that many tears. I kept looking at Steve and communicating with my eyes, are you going to do something? He would raise his hand to communicate to me to just let her cry. We sat in silence for a long time, until Steve finally led her to the only answer he truly trusted – Jesus.

Shelley: As I muddled through the next few days, I knew that it was time to make a choice. It was time to choose to own up to my weaknesses. It was time to choose to be real about that October 16th day. I knew that until I told someone, it would always be a viable option in my mind to go back to the beginning of the end. I needed some accountability. On October 26th, at 9:00pm outside of a soccer tournament in Jackson, MS, I sat in Debbie Wilson's van and said to her, "You saved me life." To which she responded in her naïve, innocent and loving way that I have come to love so much over the years, "Oh, no biggie, we love you." I said, "No, you don't understand, you really saved my life." Again, she said, "Really, its ok, we love you." What happened next will stand for the remainder of my life as one of the most profound moments I have lived. I reached over, I grabbed her by the shoulders and I said, "You don't understand, on that Thursday you came to my school, I was 5 hours away from killing myself. You, literally, saved my life." In the next moment, I watched her cry the kind of painful tears that, while I am not a parent, I am certain that only a parent can cry for a child. And I knew that I had to make the choice to get better so that I would never be the cause of the kind of pain to someone else that had been done to me.

Debbie: I felt like I had gotten hit with a ton of bricks. My initial tears were not that I had saved a life, but that I almost did not go to Shelley on that October 16th day. As we write this, I ponder what I would have felt like had I not have listened to the call of God and acted. I would have had to live with an obituary that I had been given the chance to stop. It makes me wonder, in all of our lives, how many times has God called us to be the bridge for someone and in our selfishness or lack of convenience we do not go? The reason we do not choose to be a bridge for someone else is because it causes us to have to revisit our own pain. I can remember when Shell and I were deep into the first year of working through her pain; she looked at me and said, "What about you? What about your hurts?" It was at this divine appointment, that Shelley and I both would be forced to meet adversity head on, leaving us forever changed.

Reflection for Direction

It is so easy to stay stuck in your current situation. Why? Because it is easier than the pain it "might" take to move. Our pastor is currently preaching a series called "Stuck". He shares that many people are stuck in dysfunction and addictions and refuse to move because of the familiarity of their current life circumstances. Ruth 1:14-17 speaks of Naomi who has lost her two sons, as well as her husband and as a result, is returning back to the comfort of her home. Naomi's daughters in laws decide to go with her, but along the way one of the daughters in laws wants to turn back. "At this they wept again. Then Orpah kissed her mother-in-law goodbye, but Ruth clung to her. Look, said Naomi, your sister-in-law is going back to her people and her gods. Go back with her. But Ruth replied; don't urge me to leave you or to turn back from you. Where you go, I will go and where you stay, I will stay. Your people will be my people and your God my God. Where you die, I will die, and there I will be buried." I know, I know, you are asking, "What is the relevance here?" There will always be people in our life pulling us back to the abnormal, however if we truly want to walk with God and trust Him, we must choose to move forward putting the pain of the past in perspective.

Life Talk

It is time to stop Rear View Mirror Living. We tend to continuously look back and beat ourselves up for choices we made in our lives or times when we felt we could have protected ourselves and didn't. It is time to let go of the, oh so familiar places and securities, that we have relied on for so long to get us by. It is time to stretch ourselves to new places. What old things are you holding on to and returning to that are destructive in your life? Why are you afraid to let go?

Choose Life

"For you have spent enough time in the past doing what pagans choose to do-living in debauchery, lust, drunkenness, orgies, carousing and detestable idolatry. They think it strange that you do not plunge with them into the same flood of dissipation, and they heap abuse on you. But they will have to give an account to him who is ready to judge the living and the dead." ~ 1 Peter 4:3-5

LOVE AND FORGIVE

We are all looking for love and the love we want is usually right in front of us but we are so unwilling to reach out and take hold of it. For many of us, the barrier to love and to be loved lies in our inability to forgive those who have wounded us. Steve and Debbie, those are great words, but you don't understand the pain from my father abusing me, the loss of my child due to an unnecessary death, the financial stress placed on me by another person, the devastation I felt when my mate had an affair and the lack of dishonesty from people I trusted. You are correct, we are not there and we are not living in your current circumstances, however, when we hold on to those things we were wronged by, the resentment or lack of forgiveness is like poison. The problem is that the people who wrong us are not going to be the ones taken down by that poison. We are!

What are you resentful about that you are unwilling to let go of? What is keeping you from letting go?

_____

_____

_____

I believe that many times we do not forgive because we are consumed with the fact that if we forgive we are downplaying the level of our pain thus, creating the possibility of our pain being forgotten. However, if we do not forgive, the resentment will eventually corrode our hearts. I did not realize in my own life that my heart still felt the corrosion of past hurts until the day Shelley asked me about my hurts.

Continue with us, as we journey through forgiveness.

Shelley: I was midway through the most difficult two years of my life when one morning I had the discernment that while I had hurts from the abuse and neglect I suffered, that I was not the only one dealing with past hurts. During this time, I was not sure that I could continue on with the healing until the person helping me heal also got vulnerable. So, I took the chance and asked, "What are your hurts?" The woman who had now become my most trusted ally through the course of the journey looked at me as though she was ready to slit my jugular. I thought, "Ok, maybe not a good move by me."

Debbie: It made me angry when Shell asked me about my hurts. This journey was supposed to be about her, not me. I was much more comfortable pointing out her weaknesses and her lack of forgiveness than I was looking into the magnifying glass of my own life. She was, however, relentless in her pursuit to make me dig deep. She was going no further in this journey until she knew that I was completely trustworthy and in her eyes, trust could only come through vulnerability and vulnerability could only come from emptying my heart.

Are you trying to help others without dealing with your own hurts and lack of forgiveness?

_____

_____

_____

Forgiveness is often the most difficult thing for anyone to do. It takes strength, courage and the reality that we will still be accepted if the person we are willing to forgive completely rejects us. Steve and I witnessed this first hand as we lived Shelley's hurts with her. Early on, we hammered in her, "You have to forgive your parents if you want to experience freedom."

Shelley: First of all, I began to break down walls when I recognized that the person, who had become the only Mom I knew emotionally, was not void of hurts either. I think too many times, we want to put the pain of the past on some type of scale, believing that if my pain is worse than your pain, that my pity is worthy of acceptance. Pain is pain, and while it does have varying degrees, the bottom line is that if it is not dealt with, it will steal much of our life from us. How did I deal with it? I began to take every painful memory and voice it. I laid it out there and it hurt, BAD! But I remember so vividly a statement that my adopted Dad has always used, "You will decide to heal and forgive when the pain to stay the same is greater than the pain to change." As I write this and am forced to do my best to remember the process of hurting, forgiving and then healing I immediately think of a recent ankle surgery I had. I had the surgery and woke up to realize it was worse than we originally thought. When the stitches and cast had been removed, we learned that the incision had busted open in the cast causing me four weeks of intense wound care therapy to clean up any infections that might be settling in my ankle. It hurt! But each visit to the wound care doctor made the wound and thus, the hurt better. Eventually the wound healed, yet there was still the pain of the inside healing that would eventually disappear. My heart was much the same. It hurt! My willingness to go to my biological parents and forgive them did not change my relationship with them. It did, however, change the healing on the inside of my heart. Like my ankle, I will always have a scar. But the heart scar represents the freedom I experienced from "letting go" of something that had bust open many years ago. Can I just tell you, I was truly void of love until I forgave those who wounded me? The ability to love was not instant. Eventually, though, the clouds began to dissipate and the sun shined brighter and brighter until God brought me from the place of "Why me?" to "Why not me?"

Debbie: I'm sure there were days that I rushed Shell through the forgiveness process. I think I did so because I was weary from the journey and all the sacrifices God had called me to make. I realize now that true forgiveness can not begin until the person needing to forgive has experienced a tremendous amount of healing and trust in something they can reach out and touch. Shelley did eventually go to her biological parents and forgive them and yet, it has taken time to fully heal and grow to a healthy place for her. I tell you that to help

You understand that forgiveness is a process, but if you never begin the process, you can not and will not love unconditionally nor will you ever allow yourself to be loved unconditionally.

Do you struggle to love? Would you be willing to soul search and admit that you are unable to love because someone has deeply wounded you and you have been unable to forgive them?

_____

_____

_____

As a woman, our husbands often accuse us of loving our children more than we love them, however, we subconsciously realize that our kids will not purposely hurt. The problem is this, if you want love in the purest, fullest and richest form, there is no way you will ever get it or give it until unconditional forgiveness is a part of your life.

Reflection for Direction

Forgiveness allows us to live at peace with ourselves and those closest to us. When we hold onto anger and resentment enormous amounts of energy are wasted, love is withheld and relationships are destroyed. Your lack of forgiveness may seem like it is being managed on the outside, but I am certain that your insides are being eaten alive. Shelley would try and convince me over and over that she had forgiven in her heart, but the anger and defensiveness that came from her mouth gave a clearer indication of her heart than any imaging system could have. God is calling you here and now to examine your heart and deal with any bitterness or resentment you have toward someone else or toward yourself. Let it go **today** so that you may love one another.

Life Talk

Today's life group needs to be simple, yet bold. Is there someone in this group you need to forgive? If so, stop waiting. Do you need to call an old friend and bridge the distance created in your relationship so many years ago? If so, pick up the phone and make it happen. Do you need to hold someone accountable to forgive another person who you know has wounded them deeply? Help them do that. Is it time for you and your husband to snuggle close and forgive each other for the time spent tearing each other up in your marriage? If so, get alone and pray for God's healing. Folks, we are not guaranteed tomorrow and because Jesus forgave us, it is our responsibility to forgive others.

Choose Life

"And when you pray, if you hold anything against anyone, forgive him,
so that your Father in heaven may forgive you your sins."
~ Mark 11:25

A DO OVER

"The God I believe in is a god of second chances."

Steve loves to play golf with our boys. Recently, he was playing golf with our oldest son. They walked to the 18th tee box all tied up. Josh teed off first and hit his ball in the lake. Steve tossed Josh another ball and said, "Hit another one." Josh hit a phenomenal shot into the middle of the green, putted at the hole, missed it, but tapped in for par. Steve, on the other hand, missed his putt for a bogey. Josh raised his arms in the air and said "Woo hoo, I beat you Dad." To which Steve responded, "You didn't beat me Josh, hit it in the lake." Josh said, "Dad I beat you, you gave me a Do Over and in Do Overs, the first shot doesn't count." What a cool picture of what God does for you and me. He continuously gives us Do Overs, yet the problem is that we can not and will not get over the first mistake enough to recognize that God has already forgotten about your past, he has forgotten about your mess up and he has forgotten the times you rejected him.

Have you ever been given a Do Over? What was the scenario?

_____

_____

_____

Have you ever given a Do Over? How did the other person react?

_____

_____

_____

We are all jacked up people and we are going to mess up. It is impossible not to, otherwise we would be God. Steve and I have hurt each other in our marriage. We have messed up several times and will continue to hurt one another, but the freedom to know that we so willingly give one another a second chance and a third chance has helped us accept one another and others for who they are, regardless of the mistakes they make. It creates in us an environment with a safety net of acceptance, love and forgiveness. In my journey to help Shelley we made mistakes, but jump with us to several years later as we share with you the visual of God's do over in both of our lives and in the life of our family.

Debbie: The journey to help Shelley and her healing was a very long process. For the first two years, it was like going through chemotherapy treatment for a cancer patient. However, I made some mistakes in that I allowed Shelley to become too dependent on me rather than pushing her in the direction of God. In doing this, there were times I neglected the needs of Steve, Josh, Jordan and Janae. I did not intend to do this, but it goes back to the concept that if we are not careful we sometimes have a tendency to replace great things with good things.

Shelley: In the process of the most painful years of my life, I believe that my healing did not take place as quickly as it could have because I manipulated the time and energy that Deb was willing to give to me. I selfishly did not think of anyone but myself. I wanted all the attention focused on me and my pain and I am embarrassed to admit it today, but my controlling nature, my defensiveness, my brash and ugly words, my anger and my ability to justify my needs and wants made it almost impossible for her to be honest with me. God has given me a tremendous gift of discernment and there were days that I knew in my heart, I needed to back off so that time and attention were not stolen from the rest of the Wilson family, but instead I made the choice to continue to drain the life out of them. It crushes me to willingly admit that years later, I had to go back to my siblings and ask them for forgiveness for the time I took away from them in my crisis. As much as it crushes, it also gives me great joy and humility as I think of the Do Over they each have given me. Just this past Thanksgiving, we were all sitting around the dinner table, and Mom asked the question, "What one person has had the greatest impact on your life and why?" I'm sure they were all thinking I was going to say, Mom, I mean for goodness sake, she saved my life. However, my response was Josh and this is why. He had always been the oldest child in the Wilson family and I am convinced that he felt the hardest hit from the time consumption I stole from his Mom. And yes, there were some hard times between us, but in the end he gave me a Do Over in forgiving me for that time period I took from him and he choose to love and accept me as his sister. I believe that because he did, Jordan and Janae followed behind him and in the journey through the past thirteen years it has created an amazingly sweet relationship between the four of us. Guys, one person's choice to extend a Do Over has touched and impacted the lives of our entire family.

Debbie: I think there will always be a part of me that regrets being so involved in the situation with Shelley that I was unable to see what I was doing to the rest of my family. But God is so good as he gave me the strength to place boundaries around my time with Shell. And you know, it's so ironic that the very thing she fought so hard against for the first few years of our journey, which came from her desire to hang on so tightly to us for fear we were going to abandon her, was also the very thing she desired – boundaries. I am convinced that our journey looks different from your journey and yet our need for a Do Over must be similar to yours.

God wants to give you a Do Over in the same way Steve gave Josh a Do Over and in the same way he gave Shell and I a Do Over and He is not in heaven measuring the level of your mistake to determine if you are worthy of such a second chance.

Can you accept the reality that God wants to give you a Do Over?

_____

_____

_____

Have you have been divorced and you believe God has left you? Did you have an abortion and you don't think you can ever be forgiven? Have you lost a child and you so wrongly believe it was your fault? Have you allowed your depression to take you so low that you believe you can never escape? Did you lose a loved one and have the regrets of never forgiving them? Have you made bad choices because of hurts done to you and the shame is so great that you are paralyzed? Have you been dishonest to your spouse or had an affair and you are unwilling to ask for forgiveness because you are afraid he might leave you?

Christian singer, Michael Armstrong wrote a song called "Second First Times." The song was evidently written for someone who had made the mistake of giving herself away to a man who she did not intend to marry. The theme of the song, however, is not based around the mistake she made, but rather around the bondage of fear she has allowed to take over in believing that her mistake has caused her to miss her chance for a Godly mate. Why do I mention this song? It represents the fact that all of us at some time in our life will be faced with the thought in our minds or the shame in our hearts that says, "You will never have the desires of your heart. You blew it, you messed up and there is no hope for good things." That is a lie from Satan. God continuously gives us Second First Times, Third First Times and Forty First Times. However, the choice is yours to accept them?

Reflection for Direction

When I think of a second chance, I go back to the story of Joseph. At the end of Genesis, when Jacob died, Joseph's brothers came back to ask for grain one more time. They did not believe that Joseph would feed them because their father had died and they believed he was their only leverage for Joseph to continue to do for them. Fast forward with me to present day. Society has convinced us that getting even is strength and that holding our ground is perseverance. It is impossible to have a relationship with God and hold to society's ways. In Genesis Chapter 50, Joseph gives his brothers a huge "Do Over." This should represent a picture of the precedence God has set in our lives. Genesis 50:18-21 says, "His brothers then came and threw themselves down before him. We are your slaves they said. But Joseph said to them 'Don't be afraid. Am I in the place of God? You intended to harm me, but God intended it for good to accomplish what is now being done, the saving of many lives. So then, don't be afraid. I will provide for you and your children.' And he assured them and spoke kindly to them." That, my friends is a Do Over! When was the last time you extended a Do Over to your mate? When was the last time you extended a Do Over to your children, your friends, your co-workers or your pastor? It is not too late to start the process today.

Life Talk

We have all been where we knew God wanted us to extend forgiveness. In His still small way He whispers to our hearts, "I forgive you, forgive others and become the person you were created to be." We have all needed and will continue to need grace and mercy and God continues to daily lavish it on us. Why, then is it so hard for us to extend it to one another? If we do not extend forgiveness, we will live a life void of impacting anything. Were you ever given a Do Over? Did you deserve it? What did it make you feel like? Do you understand that God's love is not based on our merit, but on the gracious cross?

Choose Life

"But you are a forgiving God, gracious and compassionate; slow to anger and abounding in love." ~ Nehemiah 9:17b

IN THE PLACE OF GOD

"I would say that the surest measure of a man's or a woman's maturity is the harmony, style, joy, and dignity he creates in his marriage, and the pleasure and inspiration he provides for his spouse" ~ Benjamin Spock

If Jesus lives in our hearts, forgiveness is not an option. It is a command. Jesus says to us in Luke 6 that we are to be merciful just as he is merciful. He warns us that if we condemn, we will be condemned, if we judge others, we will be judged and if we do not forgive, we will not be forgiven. I don't know about you and your marriage, but Steve and I do not want to live outside the will of God. We want the assurance that the strand God has created in our marriage can never and will never be broken. The world will ask, "But how can you guarantee that in a world where divorce is so prevalent and human choice runs so rampantly?" First of all, we recognize the reality that we are human beings and will always be one bad choice away from destruction. Therefore, we must build a hedge of protection and Godliness around every aspect of our relationship. We must recognize the things that can, without us even realizing it, creep their way into the weak spots of our being. We must stay on guard of the things the 6 mosquitoes can steal from us. And when all else, fails, we must constantly be reminded of our covenant we made on that altar.

Before you can even begin to live in the place of God, you must first answer the question; does Jesus live in your heart?

If the answer to that question is no, can we beg of you to go and talk to someone? Go to a pastor, a Christian friend, your Sunday school teacher, your small group leader or a Christian counselor. Do not delay in this process. If Christ has come to live in your heart, please understand that if you are unwilling to forgive your mate, you are and can not be in the place of God.

Today, in this moment together with you, your mate and God, would you be willing to first examine yourself. What is keeping you out of the place of God? Is this affecting your marriage?

_____

_____

_____

How do I know if I am in the place of God? When you have the chance for revenge, do you take it? If so, you are not in the place of God. Do you hold other's mistakes over their head? If so, you are not in the place of God. Are you unwilling to forgive because of pride? If so, you are not in the place of God. The list could continue, but the bottom line here is that if you want to figure out whether or not you are in the place of God ask yourself, "Who do I protect first? If you are in the place of God, you are protecting others first and yourself last.

In crisis, who do you protect first? Why?

_____

_____

_____

Allow me to conclude mine and Shelley's journey. Yes, we made mistakes and needed several Do Overs, but in the process of the journey, Shelley got healed, I got healed, Steve and I became closer and our family was able to experience a gratefulness that we no longer take for granted. It was not mine and Steve's plan to have a fourth child, but sometimes God, in His infinite wisdom, uses not only our pain, but the pain of others to guide us to his place. Shelley was able to experience the freedom of forgiveness from the pain inflicted on her. She was able to understand and fully grasp the reality that God was with her all along. Do you remember earlier in this study when Steve laid his head down on the floor next to hers? If you will remember, his words were, "Shell, one day you will do something in your life and you will look back on this moment and understand fully God's plan in the midst of your pain?" Shelley is now the Director of a non-profit ministry. Yes, you guessed it; she has a kid's camp. Since its birth, five years ago, we have seen almost 10,000 kids come through our facility. God loves you and he ordained this life for you, but if you are unwilling to go to the depths of pain, you will never experience the depths of the amazing life on the other side. Friends, God's word is all or nothing. We can not have one foot in the world and one foot in the kingdom and consistently live a life of forgiveness, unconditional love, grace, compassion, mercy, kindness, humility, selflessness and Godliness. Our prayer is that you will get off the fence and make the decision in this moment to go "all in" with God, your marriage and your family.

Steve and I love the movie, <u>Titanic</u>. It gives such an incredible picture of the way marriage should be. When we are young, we all want our lives to look like the picture of the older couple sitting on the park bench, seemingly more in love than ever after decades of being together. If our life is going to look that way, we must be committed to love one another enough to take the good with the bad and to truly live out, "til death do us part." Listen to the following story with us and allow your marriage the opportunity to feel the tenderness we all desire to feel with another human being.

In 1912 there was an older couple that boarded the Titanic. Their names were Isadore and Ida Strauss and you may know them by the name of their little store they started in NYC, called Macy's. On an April day in 1912, they were enjoying a well-deserved vacation aboard the Titanic. They were the picture of romance as they walked the decks of the luxury ocean liner. Late that evening, as the Titanic was making its main voyage across the Atlantic, it hit an imponderable chunk of ice under the ocean's surface. As people scrambled for safety, Isadore and Ida walked calmly on the deck assessing the situation before finally approaching a life boat in the process of being filled with women and children. As Mrs. Strauss was climbing into the life boat, she stopped, changed her mind, turned to her husband and said, "Where you go, I go." Members of the crew tried to convince her that she was making a mistake. But Ida would not listen. A crew member turned to Mr. Strauss and said, "I'm sure that because you are old, no one would object to you getting into that boat." But Isadore was as stubborn as his wife and said, "I will not go before the other men." The issue was settled, neither would go without the other and neither one would go. The older couple walked to a set of nearby deck chairs. They sat down together and they waited for the inevitable.

Let us ask you this, "How many of you would give up your seat on the life boat to sit on a deck chair with the person you love while you wait for the inevitable to happen? All of our marriages have given us something good and that should be why we do it. All marriages start out good. Couples stand at the altar so in love on their wedding day with the feeling that they are invincible. We truly believe we are going into a marriage stronger than the rivets holding the unsinkable Titanic. But somewhere along the way, we hit ice bergs that we did not see coming. We hit the ice bergs of busyness, irritability, pain of the past, financial debt, lack of sexual fulfillment, dishonesty, addictions, infidelity or any number of other things. The pain these things cause are enough to make the strongest of men and women abandon ship. But, many of us do not abandon the other because our hearts are reminded of the good and so we turn to each other and say, "Where you go, I too will go."

Reflection for Direction

One of my favorite characters in the Bible is an incredible man named Job. God allowed Satan to tempt him and it caused him to lose everything in his life. He lost his home, his animals, his children and his money. For many of us, we would have surrendered to the hurt and devastation we encountered and walked away from God. Job, however, continued to trust God. Job is best known for a statement he made after he lost everything. His wife wanted him to curse God and he replied in Job 1:21 by saying, "Naked I came from my mother's womb and naked I will depart. The Lord gave and the Lord has taken away; may the name of the Lord be praised." We sit here today with our tiny scratches or our deep scars and yet, it is no comparison to what Job or even others have experienced, and yet, they continue to praise God. They continue to stand faithful to God and because of it are able to teach others how incredible God is. As people look at your life and all that you have lost or had to deal with, what would they see? Would they see your head held high, hurting and wounded, yet still praising God? Are you representing him as faithful and trustworthy or are your actions showing people something else about God?

Life Talk

As we conclude our last life talk, go with us through a journey of your life. Would you be willing to share what it has been like? Have any of the 6 mosquitoes stolen a part of your marriage? Will you grab the can of OFF and rid yourselves of things destroying your family? Can we leave you with a final thought? I remember not only Shelley, but so many others in our lives asking us, "Where was God in my pain? How could he love me and have let that happen?" When Shelley asked me that question I struggled because I had been in church my entire life and was still unequipped to give her sound answers. Steve and I spent the next several months researching and desiring to know that answer. While we did know that God was with Shelley the entire time she living was out childhood abuse that was not a sound answer for her nor is it a sound answer for anyone in pain. One day I went to Shelley and I said, "I know where God was." She was like, "Huh?"

I said, "I know where God was when you were being abused." I continued on, "The only place I can find in the Bible where Jesus stood at the right hand of the Father was when Stephen was being stoned in Acts 7:55-56." Shelley looked at me a bit puzzled and I said, "Shell, every time you were being abused, Jesus was standing at the right hand of the Father on your behalf. Tears were streaming down his face at the pain with which you had to endure." Steve and I want to tell you the same thing. Jesus is with you. He stands on your behalf every time you hurt. He will continue to be there for you in your marriage, with your family and with your career. He is trustworthy. Can you allow yourselves and each other to let go of bitterness and resentment so that you may one day say to each other, "Where you go, I too will go."

Choose Life

"The Lord blessed the latter part of Job's life more than the first. He had fourteen thousand sheep, six thousand camels, a thousand yoke of oxen and a thousand donkeys. He also had seven sons and three daughters." ~ Job 42:12

"In my anguish I cried to the Lord, and he answered by setting me free. The Lord is with me, I will not be afraid. What can man do to me? The Lord is with me; he is my helper. I will look in triumph on my enemies." ~ Psalm 118-5-7

"And so he died, old and full of years." ~ Job 42:17

Dear Friends,

As we come to the conclusion of our first book, tears of joy and perseverance are streaming down our faces. This was a difficult journey and yet, so worth the trip. We realized in our own lives the power of reminiscing about the past and relishing in how far we have come in our own marriage and in our walk with the Lord. We will be praying for you that our stories and insights will help you in some way and that in turn, you will pass this book onto others who might not otherwise realize they need healing. Sometimes God needs to take us back to the past so that we can heal through the present and if that is your story, we pray you will journey back. Others of you may have simply gotten off track and just need us to pray for the touch of God to realize how valuable your mate is to your life. Regardless of your story, your wounds, your joys, your tragedies, please know that the passion of our lives is to invest in your marriage and your family. We would love to hear stories inspired by this study; stories of marriages reconnecting, homes being transformed, wounds being healed and lives changed by a relationship with the Almighty God. Thank you for being willing to take the journey with us.

In Awe of Him,

Steve and Debbie Wilson

For Information on Booking a Conference
To Contact Steve and Debbie Wilson
Or
For Information on Other Resources
Log On To www.marriagemattersnow.com